THE AMBASSADOR'S WIFE'S TALE

JULIA MILES.

www.eye-books.com

eye books
About Extraordinary Things Done by Ordinary People

Published by
Eye Books Ltd
29 Barrow Street
Much Wenlock
Shropshire
TF13 6EN

www.eye-books.com

Published in Great Britain 2015

British Library Cataloguing in Publication Data.
A catalogue record for this book is available from the
British Library.

Printed by CPI Group (UK) Ltd, Croydon CR0 4YY

ISBN: 978-1-903070-90-1

To Oliver and Joe, Tom, Hugh and Lucy

CONTENTS

DIPLOMATIC DEBUTANTE

"Call for you in the manager's office," the office junior announced in her nasal voice. Wondering who might have the temerity to use my manager as a conduit, I followed her to the phone and lifted the receiver.

An urbane voice said, "This is the Foreign Office Personnel Department." My heart missed a beat. Oliver was in Aden, where a postcolonial civil war was being fought. Something dreadful must have happened. The caller ignored my gasp and continued laconically, "I understand you are engaged to Oliver Miles. We thought you should get married within three months; otherwise you will have to wait three years."

I was flummoxed. "Why on earth are you telling me this?"

"Because, my dear young lady, we have posted him. He should be leaving Aden quite soon."

"Where have you posted him to?"

"Ah well, that I cannot divulge. The point is you might wish to consider handing in your notice. In fact, it might be an idea to do so at once."

It was 1967. I was 22, and in my first proper job in the marketing department of the *Daily Mirror* newspaper. It wasn't what I wanted to do. From the age of 12, I had wanted to be a social worker, but my father encouraged me to take up a post-graduate research scholarship instead. Sitting in libraries reading about the Legal Aid scheme did not suit my energetic personality and I hardly lasted a year before taking the first job I could find.

Oliver spoke fluent Arabic and had already served in numerous Middle Eastern countries before we met. When he told his parents that we were planning to get married, his father's expression turned bleak. "London School of Economics? She'll do you no good." He turned out to be wrong, because within a month of arriving in Nicosia, our first foreign post together, I was on first-name terms with half the Cyprus Cabinet and together we established one of the original LSE alumni groups that now flourish around the world.

I did as I was told and handed in my notice. In retrospect I regard this as monstrous interference, however well-meaning, but I was still very much in awe of the Foreign and Commonwealth Office (FCO). That evening I told my mother that we had less than three months to arrange the wedding. She was watching the television news.

"You'll be lucky to have a bridegroom, the way things are going out there," she remarked drily.

I started sending Oliver telegrams, asking his opinion on the wedding arrangements. This captured the imagination of the middle-aged Asian man in Farringdon Road post office, who took an active interest in the planning.

"You have white wedding?"

"No. Just a few friends for a drink."

"Champagne and cake sort of thing?"

"Yup, that sort of thing."

"Very expensive. I have daughters." He assumed a suitably hangdog expression and reached for the yellow telegram form.

What the general public might never suspect is what goes on, or used to, on the top floor of the Foreign Office building. Six eligible bachelors known as Resident Clerks – whose job was to act as duty officers covering all out-of-hours Foreign Office business – lived up there. I had been going out with one of them before I met Oliver. There was a certain frisson to be had sitting at the top of the great empty Whitehall edifice on a Saturday afternoon. If there was a crisis the girlfriends would considerately skedaddle, but usually weekends were quiet.

Often when the phone rang the duty clerk would be on the loo, or in the bath, in the big, bathroom papered in dark green. He would emerge, receiver clasped under chin, wire stretched to the limit and towel draped strategically, gesturing urgently for a notebook and pencil.

In summer we would sunbathe on the mansard roof or watch the Trooping of the Colour from the best vantage point in London. And we would drink gallons of Mateus Rose, considered rather smart in the late '60s, while cooking up a meal for whoever was around. One evening I was preparing two chicken breasts for supper with my then-boyfriend. He turned to me and said, "I forgot to tell you there are going to be three of us for supper. There's a new chap joining us – Oliver Miles, I think he's called." That is how we met. But Oliver had barely become a Resident Clerk before he was posted, complete with gun, to Aden for two years.

We kept in touch by post. After a year he promised me a love token – an Arab rug – which I eagerly anticipated. It turned out to be strips of smelly woven goat's hair roughly sewn together, nothing like the patterned Persian carpet I'd had in mind.

Oliver came back to England a couple of times for 'official talks' and on one visit, very daringly we got engaged, having known each other for a total of about two weeks the previous year.

En route to Heathrow, where he was due to fly back to Aden, and with very little time, as the shops were about to shut at Saturday lunchtime, we stopped off to buy an engagement ring. "What stone were you thinking of?" asked the proprietor, pausing in the act of pulling down the metal shutters.

"A sapphire, perhaps?"

"Good. I have two right here …"

He held out two antique rings but I couldn't decide which, or either. Under pressure of time it was agreed that I would return on Monday to collect whichever one I preferred.

"But I hope you choose the one I like," said Oliver. And that decided it.

Despite her pessimism, my mother gamely allowed herself to be jollied into arranging my wedding. When Harrods sent notice of their January sale she led me to the posh-frock department and fell upon a cream-coloured silk dress and coat, declaring it 'perfect'. She hadn't reckoned with my hefty frame and there were some horrible splitting noises as I struggled to get the garment either on or off, I didn't mind which.

"Next size up, please," my mother commanded the salesgirl, who returned saying, "We only have it in shocking pink, madam."

"That will do." She turned to me. "You weren't thinking of a white wedding, were you?"

The less fuss the better, I thought.

Oliver came home a week before the wedding with a left-hand-drive Ford saloon and an ancient alabaster head given to him in gratitude by his boss, Sir Humphrey Trevelyan, the High Commissioner in Aden.

"Could be valuable or could be the sort of thing hairdressers use to prop their doors open. I'll have to get down to the British Museum someday to see," he commented.

We got married on a freezing February day, though the watery sun managed to make an appearance as we emerged from the London University Catholic Chaplaincy. Oliver was a devout Catholic but I wasn't and had reluctantly attended 'instruction' with the Rev. Bruce Kent, of CND fame. He pointed out the problems of a mixed marriage, especially for any future children, and urged me to convert. It seemed that he may have been the child of a mixed marriage himself and somehow after a couple of sessions I ended up more or less counselling him. As a budding social worker I could never resist taking up a 'cause'.

I resisted the idea of a hired car for our wedding. "You'll have to get used to that sort of thing," Oliver rebuked me. "What on earth is there to fuss about?"

The immediate answer was that the driver could not find the Travellers' Club, so we arrived late for our own reception. When we finally got there Oliver's mother confided: "I've just greeted a rather odd character. I wasn't sure whether he was invited but I thought he might have been one of your LSE friends so I told him to go ahead and help himself."

Later, as the staff cleared up, they found a tramp blissfully asleep beneath one of the tables. I have always thought of him as a talisman, as sweeps used to be. And I cherish my mother-in-law's image of the low life I was importing from the LSE. Our wedding was altogether rather nerve-racking. Dan Davin – a novelist, publisher, and an old friend of my father's – had had too much to drink and had taken it upon himself to make the bride's father's speech. He embarked on a never-ending theme of "she shall have music wherever she goes …". Unable to stop the flow, I maintained a fixed smile as I gripped the knife ready to plunge it into the cake, but I did notice that Sir Humphrey Trevelyan had slipped away into a corner and settled down with a book.

We returned from our honeymoon to discover that the unnamed posting had been cancelled and we were to remain in London. I, of course, was unemployed. But at the same time I was given the unsettling instruction that job-hunting would be unwise as "a post might come up at any time …" So despite longing for gainful employment I enrolled on a short French course, signed up as a volunteer at Kings Cross Citizen's Advice Bureau and went shopping, all the time aware that my friends were establishing themselves in pensionable careers.

Years later we discovered that that posting was to have been to Moscow. Oliver had learned Russian in the Royal Navy and was fascinated by the Soviet Bloc. We constantly requested a posting in Eastern Europe but the nearest we got was when Oliver became desk officer for Poland after our honeymoon.

Years later another Russian posting, as Commercial Counsellor, was again rescinded. We eventually discovered that the FCO was nervous of sending Oliver to Moscow as he had twice met the spy George Blake.

They first met in Oxford when a well-dressed Blake came scouting for graduate recruits for 'the Ministry of Defence'. Oliver knew what this meant but had set his sights on the FCO and refused the offer. A year later he was in Lebanon polishing up his Arabic at MECAS, the language school run by the FCO. Blake sidled up to him and reminded him of their previous encounter, saying that at the time he had introduced himself with a false name but now wanted to be addressed by his real one. It transpired that the police were hot on his trail and they had parked him at MECAS so that they could track his movements. He was soon arrested and in 1961 sentenced to 42 years' imprisonment. In 1966, he was sprung from Wormwood Scrubs and escaped to the USSR.

After a few months in London we were invited to attend a 'Going Abroad Course' which ran for a week in the Office. Oliver declined as he had several postings under his belt. I, having nothing better to do, toddled off for five days of pep talk and stiff-upper-lip training. Unlike all the other participants, I had no posting in view. The old hands who had been recruited as helpers to the course leader were terribly *blasé* and said things like: "Before you go, do get in touch and I'll give you the address of some darling friends in Wagadugu".

The acme of the Going Abroad Course was Wednesday afternoon's security lecture. It made us feel very important. We filed into a lecture hall where a cheeky chappie with a loud check suit and a cockney accent showed us the latest fashion in spycraft. He claimed that what we were looking at had all been removed from our embassies in the USSR or Eastern Europe. We stared in amazement at tiny contraptions that had been fitted into phone receivers or electric lights or sockets and one which had been concealed under a dining table.

Then an exceedingly grand and patrician-looking man sauntered in, seated himself centre stage, and stretched out his long maroon-socked legs with a supercilious air.

"I am what you might call the Himmler of the Diplomatic Service," he introduced himself. It was impossible to concentrate on what he was telling us; his style was ineffable. At the end he called for questions so I put my hand up and everyone in front turned round to see who dared to question this Bond-like figure.

"You say we should try not to draw attention to ourselves when abroad, so please can you explain why Heads of Mission have flags on their cars and everyone drives with diplomatic plates which are instantly recognisable?"

The audience rustled.

"Anyone like to take that one?" asked Himmler.

"I'll 'ave a go," said a bald-headed man with a Yorkshire accent in the second row. "Look lady, if you've worked your backside off for 30 years in all sorts of difficult posts as I 'ave, you wouldn't say 'no' to any of the perks, would you?"

I did not quite see how a flag-bedecked car or a CD (*Corps Diplomatique*) sticker on the back bumper could be regarded as 'a perk', but I felt I'd done my bit for the day so did not push the question further.

On another occasion I enquired about shipping out a piano at the Office's expense – and discovered the answer, surprisingly, was "yes". Subsequently we did take a rather battered upright, complete with candelabras, to Saudi Arabia, which I considered added value to our rather meagre quality of life and which I sold at a profit when we left. Upon its arrival, word spread and a Dutch hippy swathed in pale mauve with matching beads mysteriously emerged to tune it, then vanished back into the desert. The piano always sounded honky-tonk and quickly went out of tune in the humid climate.

The last event of the course was the spoof 'Cocktail Party' on Friday afternoon. We had been lectured on protocol in the morning and now had to show that we could put it into practice. We waited down the corridor and – unlike any arriving guests I have ever seen – silently filed in to be introduced to a pretend HM Ambassador and his lady wife (our course tutor), who stood as a receiving party in the doorway.

We were politely offered a gin and tonic and gratefully accepted the substitute – a thick white china cup of strong Whitehall tea. We had been told that whatever else happened we had to make conversation, to be always on the look-out for someone standing alone, and never to interrupt an apparently functioning group. We were warned that we might be addressed in any language, on any subject, and that we should do the courtesy of replying in the same.

A small lady who was role playing but in real life was a very senior Ambassador's wife, introduced herself to me as Susan Small, the dress designer. We spoke haltingly of hemlines until a young man, who ultimately became High Commissioner in Delhi, interrupted. I thought I had been rescued until I realised he was jabbering away in French.

Since I had given up my job and been advised not to seek another, I had to find ways to fill my time in London. The Office, wisely promoting self-sufficiency abroad, was offering electricity and plumbing courses, for which I eagerly signed up.

"Plumbing's off, dear, but you're on the list for electricity."

I proceeded to the Women's Electrical Centre somewhere in West London. The front row of the audience was dominated by two caricatures of the traditional Ambassador's wife, a dying breed by then. One had hair thickly striped in black and white like a zebra. The other, I noticed, kept putting her jacket on and off with a slow display of the label: Jean Patou, a French couture house. On the first day they spoke exclusively to each another, looking round as if they could not believe they were in such close proximity to the *hoi polloi*. But on the second day, one of them hailed me.

"I couldn't help overhearing your conversation," she purred. "If you really are house hunting there is a darling little *bijou* period house right by us, just behind Harrods."

"Oh how kind," I replied, "but I think we are going to the country." This was a bit of a lie but I could tell that she lived in a totally different financial bracket to us.

I sat at the back with a young American woman and had the kind of giggling fits you enjoy at school. The main object of amusement was the previously mentioned *grandes dames*, who found that their long varnished nails prevented them from wiring a plug. One raised a painted claw and addressed the tutor in a strangulated accent, "A fuse? I have not heard that term. Pray explain it."

1968 was a year of revolution. Oliver's brother Francis, who worked for Imperial Chemical Industries, (ICI, now defunct), travelled extensively in the Soviet Bloc. In October of that year, following the overthrow of the Prague Spring by the USSR, our King's Cross flat was inundated by a number of young, professional Czechs, who – having fled their country – were seeking sanctuary in England. I never discovered why Francis had given them our name as a point of contact. And stupidly I didn't think of keeping a record of their names and addresses so that when I visited Prague many years later I could have looked some of them up.

There was an organisation called Diplomatic Neighbours who supported and entertained the wives of foreign diplomats in London. We lived in a flat in King's Cross and I thought I might get to know my local group. I put on my hat, as was customary, and arrived at a very smart block of flats. Indian, Iranian and German ladies clustered around the hostess, an elegant blonde, chattering about the delights and horrors of being a diplomatic spouse. I had no opportunity to introduce myself and as part of the 'home team' I had to wait until everyone had left. When I was alone with her I told her I was new to her group.

"So where do you live?" she enquired without looking at me.

"King's Cross."

"Then what on earth are you doing in the St John's Wood group?"

"There isn't one in King's Cross."

"I should think not."

I joined what was known as the Diplomatic Service Wives Association, a support group of volunteer wives with a rather genteel approach. It was established by the FCO on welfare grounds, after a wife had committed suicide abroad. The day of the annual general meeting was the day it began to dawn on me what I had let myself in for by marrying into the British Diplomatic Service. Several of us wives squeezed into the Foreign Office's ramshackle lift. It rose about 10 feet and then stopped with a distinct and decisive 'clunk'. The temperature rose.

"Nobody speak," commanded a bossy woman. "We must preserve what little oxygen we have left."

There was an emergency telephone.

"It says on the wall it doesn't work," said someone, reluctantly dialling the number. "It says it goes to the Nigerian Bank."

There was no reply. "Not surprising if it has to go all the way to Nigeria."

The second time she dialled we could hear a click as someone picked it up at the other end.

"Hello," said a deep Nigerian voice.

"We're stuck in a lift," said the woman rather feebly.

"Oh no!" replied the Nigerian voice. "By any chance would you be in the Foreign and Commonwealth Office main building elevator?"

Mrs Bossy, on the verge of panic, took a deep breath and boomed, "Just tell him to ring the front desk and get some help."

After a while there was a scrabbling noise and a quavering voice outside said, "Hello, is there anyone in there?"

Within a few minutes we were finally winched to safety. I wondered whether this example of Olympian carelessness towards staff and the public was the Foreign Office's way of doing things. As we trooped sweat-stained into the AGM, a great roar of laughter went up which Mrs Bossy acknowledged with a wave of her elbow-length glove.

After all this, I got fed up and looked for a job. I found exactly what I was looking for: a social work position with Tower Hamlets Social Services on the Isle of Dogs. After a year I was approved as a full social worker. The very same week, and after two years at home, Oliver was posted to Cyprus.

CYPRUS: KITCHEN WARS
AND TERRORIST WORRIES

Against all odds I finally managed to pass my driving test, on icy London roads, in the first week of January 1970. A couple of days later we set off by car to Marseilles to take a boat to Limassol in Cyprus via the Corinth Canal. In those days the FCO still approved that sort of travel but quite soon it was ruled that time was money and everyone began to fly. The relaxed and romantic arrival at a post by ship is now a thing of the past.

> *Dear Mum and Dad*
> *The ship is old and creaky but there are one or two interesting people aboard – two widows, a Mrs Lynch and an elegant Mrs Henderson who claims her husband was a spy catcher in the war. Also a team of Swedish acrobats who had been appearing with Frankie Howerd in Paris. Lots of people going to Israel to fight the cause – two blokes from Manchester – a chemist and an accountant who had sold up their practices to do so. And a sweet Israeli honeymoon couple who insist on sharing their wine at dinner …*

I felt as if I was a character from a Somerset Maugham story and briefly grew in self-importance. This was quickly disabused. As the ship docked at Limassol I went down to the cabin to make myself look like how I imagined a newly arrived diplomatic wife should look: suit, heels, jewellery. Our welcoming party, Kieran Prendergast, the political Second Secretary at the High Commission (which is what Embassies are called in Commonwealth countries), and his wife Joan, leapt aboard from a rocking launch attired in shorts and sandals.

I felt very starchy next to them but our friendship was sealed immediately as we discovered that not only had our car radio been left on throughout the voyage so that the battery was flat and the vehicle had to be dragged from the boat by a Turkish tractor, but that all our worldly goods, including books, blankets and wedding presents, had been submerged in sea water in the leaky hold. To complete the trio of misadventures, we found, once we reached Nicosia, that the keys to our house had been mislaid.

With typical panache Kieran resolved the various domestic problems while Joan chatted away, serving us endless cups of tea, coffee, coca cola – and, as day turned to night – gin. In the end, exhausted, we fell into bed.

Before we had left England, I met a journalist who put the wind up me by saying that while I was abroad I should never drive over so much as a paper bag lying in the road in case it was an unexploded bomb. Cyprus had endured some years of EOKA-led terrorism until General Grivas successfully expelled the British colonial power in 1960. The Greek and Turkish governments then negotiated an agreement allowing their national contingents of soldiers to be stationed in Cyprus. These were usually young conscripts whose handling of weapons was a bit unreliable. We were once stopped at a checkpoint where the spotty teenage Turkish guard put his rifle muzzle through the car window at such an angle that the trigger caught on his trouser pocket. Alarmingly, he tugged to release it and we thought our heads might be blown off. Perhaps it wasn't loaded.

In 1960, thick 'Green Lines' dividing the Turkish and Greek communities in all the major towns had been drawn on a map by the British Chief of Staff using a Chinacraft pen. The lines were sufficiently wide as to be imprecise. The potential for dispute was readily taken up and in 1963 fighting broke out between the Cypriot populations. The UN was called in to establish and maintain peace.

By the time we arrived, the island was enjoying an uneasy stability, but heaving with callow youths from mainland Greece and Turkey and burly UN professionals from Canada, Denmark and Finland, all armed to the teeth. Our posting was marked by Greek-on-Greek fighting, notably an attempt on President Makarios' life days after our arrival. General Grivas was back on the island, in hiding. We often heard gunfire or bombs.

As diplomats, we could drive freely across the Green Line at any checkpoint. Turks could move in and out of the Greek areas, but not the other way round. So to reach northern Cyprus, across intervening territory occupied by the Turkish Cypriots, Greek Cypriots had to join the UN convoy which once a day wound its way slowly in a large loop west and north of Nicosia. Ledra Street, the main thoroughfare in Nicosia, ended abruptly in a checkpoint. The Ledra Palace Hotel, so essential to much social life, directly adjoined the Green Line on the Greek side.

My first experience of conflict occurred early one morning in the first week of March 1970. Oliver woke me up saying he had heard gunshots and an explosion, which he thought might have been a bomb. His first instinct was to run into town to see what was happening. Being new to diplomatic life I told him he was probably dreaming that he was still in Aden. My incorrect view prevailed.

Tim Daunt, the First Secretary, did go to see what was happening, and phoned us with the news that Archbishop Makarios' helicopter had been brought down. Makarios had miraculously survived, as the pilot, despite being shot in the stomach, deftly landed in a narrow street in the Old Town.

How the rotor blades avoided the power lines that criss-crossed the 20-foot-wide street, will never be known.

According to our maid, who lived on this street, the Archbishop had dragged the pilot out shouting for a taxi until eventually a sweet-and-nut stall holder took them to hospital in a clapped-out van. Our neighbour, Michael Triantafyllides, visited Makarios later that morning and told us that he was cool as a cucumber and apparently quite unscathed by his experience.

One of the men arrested for this murder attempt was the ex-Foreign Minister. Like many Cypriots he kept a stash of weapons but protested that the arms had been given to him by Makarios. The ex-Minister of Defence, Polycarpos Georgadjis, was murdered a week later. He was suspected of being an instigator of the plot against Makarios, but in the way of Middle Eastern political intrigue, although everyone 'knew' he was guilty, it remained unclear who had done what.

Dear Mum and Dad
Today we hear Georgadjis has been shot dead. He was accused by Makarios of the assassination attempt and it's been evident for some time that Mak. wanted to get rid of him. We don't know whether it was the police or a long-standing feud or what. He always protested his innocence and was supposed to be the most popular leader of the most popular party. Mind you, he had been an EOKA gunman. I hope you are not getting nervous at home; I find reading reports in The Times terrifying but living here is entirely different ... the emphasis is changing to internal Greek troubles, no longer Turk and Greek ... my Greek teacher, a left-wing Athenian, says the Brits and Americans are behind it ...

A few weeks later Oliver wrote to my parents:
We're keeping our fingers crossed over the Cyprus problem. No more shootings – the main news now is illegal arms being handed in under an amnesty. Extraordinary country

> *– one can understand a chap keeping the odd pistol or*
> *rifle but not rocket launchers and anti-aircraft guns …*

Superficially, the living was easy, but there was an underlying tension. The threat in our time was not towards the British. For that reason we were all rather taken aback one hot afternoon when a mini-terrorist put a bomb against the front door of the British High Commission and started a fire. Fortunately, the damage was not great and the Military Attaché, awoken from his siesta, extinguished it, wearing pyjamas.

The Greek Cypriots called the island '*o omphalos*' which means 'the navel', because they considered it to be the centre of the world. It certainly was not immune to international politics. When the colonial period ended in 1960 the British government retained an intelligence listening post at Ayios Nikolaos and the Sovereign Base Areas at Akrotiri and Dhekelia because of their strategic position in the Mediterranean. These bases have been used mostly as military training grounds but for us in the High Commission, they were also a reassuring source of medical care.

Cyprus has been a sanctuary and sometimes a terrorist convenience. Towards the end of 1970 civil war broke out in Jordan ('Black September'). As a result, several hundred British nationals were evacuated via Nicosia. The High Commission wives were put on alert to receive the women and children, who came out first. We waited all day until the first plane landed late in the evening. Peter Ramsbotham, the High Commissioner, went aboard to welcome them. It was one of his more lugubrious performances.

As he embarked on a short history of the island, Alan Hathaway, an ex-Royal Marine and a relatively junior member of staff, nipped under his arm shouting, "All those with names A-M turn left out of the aircraft. Follow me NOW." Mr Ramsbotham, being an amenable fellow, abandoned his speech. Soon we were dispensing as much comfort and aid as we could to the shocked families who had left their menfolk behind, arriving only with the clothes they stood up in.

Towards the end of our posting, in October 1972, Cyprus allowed a Lufthansa aircraft that had been hijacked by al Fatah, the Palestine terrorist group, to land at Nicosia for refuelling. The plane was travelling between Damascus and Frankfurt, but ended up in Libya. The hijacking was an attempt to free three Palestinians who had been imprisoned following the massacre of several members of the Israeli team at the Munich Olympics.

On another occasion the Palestinians attempted an attack on the Israeli Embassy in Nicosia. It was thwarted by a solitary Cypriot policeman. The terrorists then made for the airport intent on hijacking a plane but three of them were killed and one arrested. On each occasion I could hear a cacophony of sirens screaming down the airport road, which was one block away from where we lived.

One evening an American diplomat said to me, "I have a solution to the world's problems."

"What's that?"

"Give Cyprus to the Palestinians and you've solved the whole thing." If only there was such a slick solution.

It was scary to be so close to all this violence. It made me aware that in 1968 when I had married into the diplomatic service, some fundamental changes were occurring both at home and abroad, changes which would directly affect our lives. First came hijacking and terrorism. Like most diplomatic families we were constantly faced with the problem of security. Abroad, Embassy property began to be treated as a first line of attack by increasingly violent insurgents. Individual diplomatic personnel, traditionally accorded respect and deference by the host country, often became pawns in international squabbles – in the worst cases as victims of kidnapping or even assassination. Diplomats' children flying unaccompanied between post and school became a source of anxiety for mothers waving them off from foreign airports.

One British diplomatic child disappeared for a couple of days in Beirut because the fighting in the Lebanese civil war had closed the airport. (He was found on the beach in the company of a British Airways stewardess who had no way of informing the distraught parents that he was safe.) In Athens, the local British Embassy Prep School pupils sported bright red blazers that could have made them easy targets for kidnappers as they stood at the roadside waiting for the school bus.

A second major change was to the finances of the FCO. One of the economic measures taken by Edward Heath in 1970 was the establishment of the Central Policy Review Staff (popularly known as the 'Think Tank'), where the remit was to look at ways to cut government spending. A posse of the Great and the Good appointed to this task visited us in Nicosia. They spent a week sucking their teeth at what they regarded as our lavish style of living but which we maintained was necessary for the job of representing our country overseas.

Having visited a number of posts they came up with a series of recommendations. One was that diplomatic property should be rented, not owned, which fortunately has mostly been ignored, to the benefit of the Exchequer. The government decided to systematically cut the British diplomatic service finances by at least one percent every year, gradually eroding services. Staff in difficult postings, such as Saudi Arabia, struggled to fulfil day-to-day functions through lack of transport and other facilities. To put the savings in context, it is useful to know that the entire, world-wide British diplomatic service totalled 6,000 employees, mostly locally engaged and far fewer than in many local UK authorities.

A third influence was feminism. This was gradually gaining traction in the United States during the 1960-1970s, until it finally reached the UK. The patriarchal FCO refused employment to female diplomats if they married before 1973, and has always depended on the usefulness of compliant wives. Feminism made me question my role and gave me some confidence to assert my rights and that of other diplomatic wives. I am sure that I gained a reputation for being 'difficult' which I would argue was unjustified in view of all my committed hard work over 28 years supporting Oliver's activities.

On my first morning in Cyprus as a proper diplomatic wife I awoke to *Lilliburlero*, the signature tune of the BBC World Service, which became a familiar theme during our time abroad. Pottering downstairs I found the table laid for breakfast with a linen cloth and Ellie, the not-so young Cypriot maid, eager to discover what sort of people she had contracted herself to. Her demeanour suggested that she was tough and hardworking and did not suffer fools gladly.

As soon as breakfast was over and I had dressed, Ellie made the first move, producing a pile of folded cotton ladies' drawers, bequeathed by her favourite employer. She said she had been forced to use them as dusters by my stingy predecessor. She was hoping for something better from me.

Then she directed me to go and borrow the neighbour's Hoover. It had all been arranged, she assured me. Reluctantly I went next door and rang the bell. A puzzled-looking servant answered the door and with some difficulty – as I did not then speak Greek, I explained my mission. She indicated that I should sit and wait. I waited for a very long time. I could hear quite a lot of bumping and shouting from upstairs.

Eventually I crept home empty-handed to a contemptuous Ellie. How could she clean the house when all she had were Lady So-and-So's knickers? I slunk away to unpack but not for long as she kept me on the run the whole morning. It transpired, when I did eventually meet my neighbours, that the lady of the house had been otherwise occupied that morning – giving birth to a son. Her husband became the Cypriot Foreign Minister.

On that first day, Frances Ramsbotham, the High Commissioner's wife, had invited me to lunch with some local ladies to introduce me as the wife of the new Head of Chancery (Oliver's job title). Margaret Worsnop, an old hand, offered to accompany me to the Residence. When she arrived she looked startled at my dishevelled appearance.

"You look as if you've been working hard."

"Ellie keeps sending me out on missions and it's very hot."

"Ignore Ellie. She's a tyrant, we all know that. Oh, hello Ellie ..."

I seized the bunch of flowers for my hostess and we set off across the Green Line to the pretty Turkish villa that served as the High Commissioner's Residence.

In each post the Residence is where the Head of Mission lives, whether he is called Ambassador or High Commissioner. The building, sometimes historic and palatial, is used for official entertaining and putting up visiting dignitaries such as members of the Royal family, government ministers, members of Parliament, captains of industry etc. but it can also be just a flat, like the Residence in New York where the Ambassador to the United Nations lives. In Cyprus there was a Residence on each side of the Green Line.

The reason for this was that while living in the Turkish villa the High Commissioner and his wife had suffered a personal tragedy. They had lost confidence in their surroundings and had had the villa exorcised twice. So they preferred to reside in a small villa on the Greek side, where they usually entertained.

As I was the guest of honour, we were the first to arrive – as I had been taught on the Going Abroad course – but I had hardly said a word to my hostess before the other women guests, both Cypriot and British, came trooping in and lunch was announced. We sat down to a plate of finely chopped lettuce. Odd, but we chomped our way through it. The second course was chopped lettuce, too.

"Wow, Frances," said Irene, an outspoken blonde who ran the St John's Ambulance, "you are so good to consider our figures."

Mrs Ramsbotham blenched but acknowledged the compliment with a slight incline of her head. The pudding was a sort of liquid lemon froth.

As staff wives we had to remain behind until everyone had left. "Thank you so much," I started to say.

"Oh my dear," she interrupted, tossing her girlish pony tail. "If only you knew. I got home at ten to one, to find the cook in bed with the sheet over his head. So I just went into the kitchen and chopped. Luckily, he had begun making the lemon sorbet."

"It was a memorable occasion," I said, truthfully.

In the car Margaret remarked, "She passed it off so graciously, nobody would have suspected what had happened." I resolved to try to do the same.

I had hardly returned home when the phone rang. It was our neighbours, Dolly and Michael Triantafyllides, who became very dear friends. Michael was appointed Chief Justice during our time. Dolly came from a wealthy East African Greek family and while imperious in manner she was also kind.

"We want you to come over this evening so that we can meet you."

This put me in a difficult situation; I could not ask to what exactly we were being invited. My parents-in-law had once answered such an invitation expecting a meal but received brandy and a cigar instead. Oliver was underwhelmed by my ineptitude.

"How could I say 'is it for dinner'?" I retorted.

"Well, now we don't know whether to eat or not."

After we had consumed some pork chops we crossed the road.

"Hello!" said Michael warmly, shaking our hands. "So pleased you could join us for our little buffet." It was a Roman feast.

The High Commissioner and his wife were assiduous, if rather preoccupied hosts. The food was never very good but the Ramsbothams were kind and generous and you never knew whom you might meet at their parties which, often being impromptu, could descend into theatre. One morning Oliver phoned me at about 11am to say that there was to be a lunch at the Residence. It did not augur well.

"Can you think of anyone we can place between the head of MI5 and a journalist from the Economist Intelligence Unit?

Unfortunately they are both coming today." The head of MI5 at the time was Sir Martin Furnival-Jones.

The dining table had been extended to its maximum length and a large vase of flowers strategically placed. The guest list had been doubled to include two lady majors who lived in a cave (and in 1974 single-handedly saw off some Turkish invaders). A few others had been dragged in, including Mr Ramsbotham's social secretary who was probably responsible for this muddle. Gil Morris, an undercover intelligence officer and therefore possibly one of Sir Martin's staff in the High Commission, and his wife were necessarily present.

I sat on the left of Peter Ramsbotham with Gil on my left and Sir Martin opposite. I could sense Oliver at the other end of the table parrying questions from the journalist. As lunch was served, Gil sang loudly and tunelessly, "Who could want for anything other than Mrs Ramsbotham's lamb chops?" But nobody heard as noise levels were elevated.

I noticed Mr Ramsbotham kept dropping cutlery, napkins and lamb bones onto the floor, possibly from nerves. Sir Martin sat impassive and silent throughout, but as we rose from the table I saw that a zigzag mark like the sign of Zorro had appeared right across his forehead. I have no idea how it got there or whether it held any significance, and it was impossible to ask.

After a decent interval to become socially acclimatised, it was our turn to issue an invitation to the High Commissioner and his wife. This was a truly scary moment and needed planning.

"Mrs R. will insist you sit with her before dinner so don't think you can go into the kitchen," warned a friend.

At our dinner parties Alexi, a dim but well-meaning post office messenger, served the food and washed up afterwards. We liked him because he was outside the catering mafia run by Pieris, an unpleasant-looking man who boiled vegetables with bicarbonate of soda to keep them looking green. However, since I wanted all to go smoothly, I booked Pieris weeks ahead, periodically checking that I was in his diary. I wanted him to put the finishing touches to the meal that

I would have already prepared. On the afternoon of the dinner he informed me that he had a pressing engagement elsewhere and was sending his highly recommended 'best man' instead.

Neither Pieris nor any of his random henchmen were trained. They were blue-collar workers by day who metamorphosed into waiters and kitchen staff around 6pm. Best Man's appearance caused me a momentary spasm. A deep scar ran diagonally across his face and he looked like a thug. With no time to spare I took him into the kitchen.

"Who's that?" Alexi asked in a whisper.

"Pieris says he's great." I said firmly. Alexi looked unconvinced.

Best Man was a swashbuckler. "Leave everything to me," he cried, flinging out his arms like a tenor. "Alexi and I will do everything."

Just as predicted, Mrs Ramsbotham positioned herself at the senior lady's end of the sofa and patted the seat next to her. "Come and sit next to me, my dear."

I felt an urge to check how things were going in the kitchen but couldn't. Alexi announced that dinner was served. The dining table was adorned with a linen cloth but nothing else. We waited quite a long time, the conversation eventually dropping to a murmur. Ignoring Oliver's meaningful look, I went into the kitchen, where Best Man had Alexi's head in an arm lock, and a knife at his throat. Tears rolled down Alexi's cheek.

"He's put the soup on the meat," he sobbed.

"Well, just tip the soup off the meat and serve it," I said.

It was thick, greasy and congealed. "Delicious," the High Commissioner announced, in his *basso profundo*.

"Oh, Mr Ramsbotham ..." I started to say in a querulous voice.

"Don't tell me now."

We were expected to entertain as much as possible, limited only by our entertainment allowance and the amount of energy and commitment that I, as cook and hostess, could summon up. This probably meant not less than a couple of formal meals each month as well as frequent drinks parties and small suppers. After a couple of years of sweating it out in the kitchen, I was required to lay on a buffet for 60 people. All morning I singlehandedly hauled tables and chairs from the British Council. As I stood stirring something over a very hot stove in the very hot kitchen, with a toddler balanced on my pregnant belly, the penny dropped: What the hell was I doing? I didn't graduate from the LSE to become an unpaid domestic servant.

But there was no let-up. There was no financial allowance for a cook even if we could have found one in Cyprus. The Foreign Office loftily exploited the diplomatic wives' good nature, and any complaint to the Diplomatic Service Wives Association was met with, "It's for the love of your husband". Once, at an AGM in London, I suggested that the FCO sent out pre-cooked frozen meals to posts. This won a round of applause but in reality there was no escape from the hard work of entertaining.

The meagre supply of cultural events meant we were thrown back on our own resources, so people were always trying to make their parties different and memorable. The Americans played party games which became increasingly *risqué* as the night wore on. The German Second Secretary once papered over the doors and windows of his dining room while we guests were eating, to see if we became disorientated. The French Ambassador only served you pudding once you had answered an ancient riddle inscribed on your plate.

But it seemed to me that entertaining was so full of possible pitfalls (I once chopped up cards for place names and Michael Triantafyllides flipped his over to discover 'Vote Labour' embellished in red capitals on the back) that I was not deliberately going to increase the risk of something going wrong.

On the occasion of a big birthday party in a nice restaurant Oliver felt ill and went home but I decided to stay. My heart sank when I was directed to sit next to the dreary old Minister of Commerce, inevitably an alumnus of the LSE. To my amazement he asked me to dance. As we twirled about he asked if I had locked my car.

"No, I never lock anything in Cyprus."

He came to a halt. "Then you are very foolish. You never know."

We resumed dancing. After a while he remarked, "I hope you haven't noticed that we keep going straight and I never turn round?" I hadn't.

"I just want to tell you that I am keeping you between me and Nicos Sampson."

I glanced over my shoulder and froze, because there sat the EOKA terrorist and murderer himself, amiably chatting away.

Sometimes friendly efforts to help a party along had unexpected results. David Beattie, the High Commission First Secretary, and his wife Ulla entertained on Thursdays. One night as we ate our first course the conversation took a while to get going. A kindly Greek Cypriot dentist, desperately wanting to help, indicated a portrait which hung over the fireplace.

"Is that your grandfather?" he enquired.

"No," said David grimly. "It's King Charles I."

Before another Thursday function, David briefed me on my dinner partner:

"He's an Archimandrite – a monk in the Greek Orthodox Church. They should be unmarried and celibate but this one has two teenage children. Everybody in Cyprus knows, but don't say anything. Do you understand?"

We reached the knife clattering, sticky conversation stage. I had been learning Greek, so after thinking through the necessary vocabulary, I turned to the bearded figure on my left and enquired in Greek: "How did you become a priest?" The whole table exploded with laughter, including the Archimandrite who said, "The word you are looking for is *pappas*. Not 'papa'."

One of our Cypriot friends invited us to a Christmas dinner party. As I queued up at the buffet, I looked round to see where I might sit. At the furthest table, all by himself, sat a bald, pasty-faced man in a rather nasty brown suit. He seemed lonely so with my plate piled high, I asked whether I might join him.

"No problem."

"Oh, I think I detect an American accent."

"That's right. I live in Los Angeles – well, Hollywood actually."

"So perhaps you are in the film business?" I fished.

He regarded me suspiciously. "You could kinda say that."

I became aware that everyone else was watching us. It seemed odd but there was nothing I could do about it so I ploughed on asking about his roles and films. He looked closely at me as if checking whether I was winding him up.

"Cops and robbers, this and that," he answered.

Then some latecomers arrived. They came over to our table. "Hi, Telly, how are you doing, man?"

They hugged and slapped each other on the back. Turning to me they said, "So you've had the great man all to yourself. Count yourself lucky."

I was still mystified, which must have showed.

"Telly Savalas – *Kojak* – you must know."

I grinned wanly. I honestly did not know. We had no television and it was only after asking around that I understood that my Cypriot-born dinner partner was a big celebrity.

ON HER MAJESTY'S FREQUENT SERVICE

We made friends from both the Greek and the Turkish communities, privately feeling sorry for the Turks in their impoverished enclave. On their side of the Green Line we could buy handmade leather shoes for little more than pennies and the High Commission men had suits expertly run up by Turkish tailors for a fraction of the cost back home.

The Turks themselves were a proud and friendly lot. Patricia Daunt, whose house we inherited when she and her husband Timothy left Nicosia soon after we arrived, got hold of me at dinner one night.

"Look, you've got a duty to keep in touch with the Turkish women. Do you play bridge?"

"Not at all."

"That doesn't matter. I'll call for you tomorrow and introduce you to Mrs Rustem and Mrs Kucuk and the others if they come."

Mrs Rustem, the wife of the owner of the only bookshop in Nicosia, was the hostess. We had to drive across the Green Line to reach her house, which was a large sandstone edifice standing in a dusty unpaved street that looked distinctly run down. Citrus fruit was hanging by her front door. A buxom woman in her thirties with dyed blonde hair, Mrs Rustem, was leaning against the door jamb as we drew up.

"Have you seen the maiden's breasts?" She giggled, fondling one of the fruits dangling from the tree. "They are much bigger than grapefruit."

She welcomed Patricia warmly and eyed me appraisingly. "What convention do you play?"

I looked at Patricia helplessly.

"Julia is just a beginner but very keen to replace me on Wednesday mornings. Aren't you?" She gave me a basilisk stare.

"Er, well I suppose so. I certainly want to get to know some Turkish women."

They all laughed. "Why don't you partner Madame Kucuk?"

"Blimey," I thought to myself. "She's the Vice-President's wife."

Mrs Rustem placed herself to the right of me in front of a china cabinet and flipped a pack of cards with manicured hands, nails shining like shells. She held them out to me.

"No dear, you are not supposed to take them but to shuffle them."

I began to sweat. I had no idea what I was doing and this quickly became obvious to all.

Finally Mrs Kucuk complained, "She has no idea; she's just trumped my ace."

"I win," declared Mrs Rustem.

"You invariably do," retorted Patricia. "I always wonder how you do it."

"She sits in front of that mirror," replied Mrs Kucuk, indicating the mirror-backed china cabinet.

"Not only that," cried Mrs Rustem gaily, and pulled out a third pack of cards which she had hidden under the table.

At that moment the maid brought in a selection of creamy sweetmeats. We fell upon them greedily, if only to regain some sort of equilibrium.

One day late in our posting we decided that instead of the usual carefully segregated entertaining we would throw a party for both communities, as we had a gut feeling they would get along. It was a great success. Greeks and Turks embraced with tears in their eyes, reminiscing to anyone who would listen. The next day Ellie suddenly confessed a long-held secret: she had a twin brother who had been adopted as a baby by a Turkish family. They had not had any contact since. We were sure that the political division did not reflect the true differences between the populations at all accurately, and on a human level it was insupportable.

The two communities came together again at the annual Queen's Birthday Party (QBP). This was held in the garden of the Ledra Palace Hotel, because the High Commissioner's Residence on the Greek side of town was too small and his Residence on the Turkish side was inaccessible to the Greeks. Much time and effort was taken by the High Commission staff in its planning.

One challenging task was compiling the guest list, with invitations much sought after. Although it was aimed at the local population and other diplomatic missions, a large number of 'Ancient Britons' had to be accommodated, too. These were British people, mostly retired, numbering then about 10,000, who had emigrated to Cyprus. Many made supreme efforts to ingratiate themselves with the High Commission. As the QBP hove into view there was intense speculation and competition amongst them about who had received the embossed invitation card.

The two Misses Smith, both aged over 80, hit on an unfailing plan. They presented themselves, dressed to the nines in floral silk and battered old hats, and simply gate-crashed. When one of them collapsed and was carried to a cool spot elsewhere in the gardens to recover, she was seen shortly afterwards tottering through the entrance again. Nobody had the heart to stop her.

A British military band was appointed to play the National Anthems. This was a moment of exquisite diplomacy: should both the Turkish and the Greek anthems be played? Someone suggested that each anthem be played in proportion to the area of land they covered, or the size of their population. Wars have started for less.

Precedence was also a headache. One year Prince Michael of Kent was invited because he was serving as a junior officer with the British contingent of the UN Peacekeeping Force. His commanding officer was also invited, as well as Archbishop Makarios and the Vice-President, Mr Kucuk. How could the time of their arrivals be staggered to take account of rank? These were not trivial questions.

The High Commission wives were subjected to a pep talk on appropriate QBP dress and behaviour. One year, consternation ran across the island as the death of the Duke of Gloucester was announced. Would the QBP be cancelled? Not on your nelly. But Court Mourning was ordered.

"What exactly does that mean?" I asked Oliver.

"Just wear black."

"I haven't got anything black."

"Well, that was a bit short-sighted of you. Didn't the Post Report suggest diplomatic staff have black clothing to hand at all times?"

"It might have, but I thought I'd risk it. I've found a dark blue frilly chiffon blouse, but moths seem to have got into one arm."

"Just paint your arm black. No one will notice the holes in the dark."

"Brilliant suggestion. Where's the ink?"

Three months after arriving in Nicosia we moved from the gloomy house that we had been allocated into a lighter, brighter place round the corner. I made a request for new sitting-room curtains as the existing ones were completely rotten. When I tried to draw them, only a tattered two-inch strip budged and a shower of jolly little geckos with the consistency of rubber bands rained down on my head. Months later, some Home County floral curtains arrived, which were a great improvement.

Foreign cookers often proved problematic. For an anxious hostess like me bottled gas was worrying because there was no way to know when it would run out. Anticipating imminent pitfalls, I invited Matthew, the High Commission handyman, to demonstrate how to attach the rubber tube to a full bottle. Matthew was well meaning but none too bright and ran a lighted match round the top of the casing of one of the gas cylinders "to see if it was safe". He had also hung my new curtains inside out "so that people in the street could admire them".

It was only a matter of time before I found myself in a chiffon evening dress rolling cylinders round the garden in search of a full one. I was conscious of the guests gathered in the drawing room, including the High Commissioner and his wife who were, I hoped, unaware of my struggle to cook their dinner, until I made a dishevelled entrance from the garden.

As a diplomatic wife it was no use complaining; whinging was frowned upon and requests for equipment were routinely ignored. We asked for some bookshelves but were dismissed peremptorily with the statement that we already had the 2.5 metres allowed for our grade. So we ended our career with a motley collection of bookcases bought from our own pocket. The one from Saudi Arabia had gold edges.

When we left Cyprus after three and a half years, the young Administration Officer came to do the inventory. She stood for a while in our bedroom.

"Is that the bed you've been sleeping in all this time? It's terribly narrow." (I forebore to say that I fell out of it regularly.)

"Now you know why we keep having children," I said. She didn't find it funny.

We arrived in Nicosia childless and left as a family of four. When I first became pregnant I felt apprehensive about having a child abroad, even though the Foreign Office guarantees to provide healthcare of an NHS standard to families abroad. In Cyprus they had negotiated a maternity contract with the British Military hospital at Dhekelia, about 40 miles from

Nicosia. My baby was due on Boxing Day 1971, which seemed a rotten birthday, so I decided to grit my teeth and hang on.

On Christmas Day the car had a puncture and I wondered how I would get to hospital. Oliver indicated that he had a plan, and later that morning reported total success. He had taken the car across the Green Line where, of course, Christmas was not being celebrated. A cheerful Turkish-Cypriot mechanic had said in a cockney accent, which he could only have picked up in North London, "What's 'appening over there then? Easter or somefing?" and mended the puncture in a twinkling.

I arrived at the hospital on New Year's Day to be greeted by a crashing sound reminiscent of the Duchess' kitchen in Alice's Wonderland.

Loud British female voice: "Mrs Georgiou, stop that at once."

Crash, smash. "Mrs Georgiou. I've warned you ..."

Then a deathly silence followed by "Awa, awa, awa ..."

"What on earth is going on?"

"Oh it's just one of them Cypriots, they always do that," explained my hospital escort.

I wondered whether Mrs Georgiou had been wheeled fully dilated into the delivery room clutching a pile of saucepans. How else might she have produced those sound effects? After the dreaded enema and what might now be called a full Brazilian, I was forced to eat a greasy fry-up. It seemed a strange meal to serve to a woman whose body's priority was not digestion. It turned out that the hospital helper who pre-ordered meals for new patients delighted in choosing the least suitable. I noted her sadistic activity and warned others about her.

"You'll need all your strength," commanded the Queen Alexandra Royal Army Nursing Corps lieutenant, standing over me. There was no arguing with a QARANC nurse, especially one whose triangular starched headdress made her look like a cross between a manta ray and an angry nun. It proclaimed: don't mess with me or else.

Two days of intermittent labour and many salt baths later, baby Joe arrived as the sun came up on 3 January, 1972.

Obstetric-Major Lees dropped by in full riding kit. I mistook his riding crop for forceps and, according to impeccable witnesses, shouted "Take that bloody thing away". At which moment Joe's head crowned.

Since this was a military hospital everything had to be done by the clock. Five hours after giving birth I was turfed out of bed and the bedclothes stripped; I was ordered to remake it with hospital corners. Turning a heavy-duty hospital mattress made me feel as if I was being rent asunder. Even climbing into the high bed was torture as the episiotomy stitches yawed this way and that. Finally I flopped back onto my pillow. But the physio was on her way up and Sister turfed me out again. "Tsk, Tsk, you can't lie there all day, my girl," she reprimanded me.

I was lying in bed when the doctor came round and I tried to tell him about my aches and pains. Sister stood behind him and gestured to me with a snapping movement of her fingers to keep my mouth shut. After the ward round she came back. "You are not permitted to speak to the doctor unless you have put in a request in writing 24 hours in advance. And when the Major comes in you must lie to attention with nine inches of sheet folded down and your arms outside the blankets." I thought she was joking.

As I began to move around and mix with the 'other ranks' wives in the big ward next door, I realised, despite the notice hanging over my bed denoting me as 'a non-entitled civilian', how privileged I was. They were as compliant as one might expect soldiers' wives to be. Dressed in see-through pastel-coloured baby-doll pyjamas, they ran around at Sister's command tidying the ward, bathing their babies and, rather comically, standing to attention next to their beds when the Obstetric-Major visited.

I made friends with Kerry, who was disappointed at having a third son. "We're thinking of calling him Glen. Nice with Warren and Dale, don't you think?"

"I think it's a perfectly idyllic name …"

We took it in turns, in our nightwear, to wheel the heavy lunch trolley onto the ward and distribute the individually plated food, which was covered with battered aluminium lids. There was always an argument.

"I never ordered fish."

"OK, who ordered fish?"

"Can't stand the stuff – even the smell makes me heave …"

"OK, so who ordered fish?" Silence.

"It was that cow who orders the greasy stuff for the new patients."

I had silently thought the same. "OK, I'll have the fish this time. Who ordered the hamburger?" And so on it went.

At bedtime, cocoa was served; I suppose this is what the Army did in the field. It was an unexpected perk but caused huge problems later because Sister had forbidden us to move after lights out. It was more than my life was worth to nip to the loo. Three hours later and there was nothing to do but to pee in my empty cocoa mug, tip it into the basin and hope it would be well washed up.

Sixteen months later, I was back for a second delivery. A different doctor and a new regime. Major Lees' replacement, Colonel Brown, peered over his half-moon specs:

"Mrs Miles, it is my professional opinion that you should come into hospital immediately. General Grivas is going to blow up the road and we don't want Baby born in a hedge, now do we?"

I thought to myself: "I've met wives who claim to have dropped their babies behind thorn bushes in the Jordanian desert." But instead replied: "My husband is the Embassy Political Secretary and I don't think he would agree with you."

"Bring him with you next visit," he smiled, indicating that the examination was over.

When I recounted this conversation to Oliver he said, "I'm absolutely confident you will be able to get to hospital. There's no reason to think Grivas is going to mine the road. Why should he?"

"Well you come and tell the quack. He might listen to you."

To my surprise, Oliver did accompany me on my

subsequent visit. It was a treat not to have to drive the 80-mile round trip by myself in the searing heat. He and Colonel Brown looked like two rutting stags walking in circles, eyeing each other before locking horns. Finally the doctor held up his hands in a gesture of submission. "Well, if that is your considered opinion ..."

Grivas obligingly concentrated on other targets and I got to hospital, where a meaty-looking doctor announced that he would induce me. By turning a tap on the drip he could time the delivery. There was another woman in labour so it was decided that – in order to fit some military timetable – I should deliver at ten to noon and she at ten past.

But I knew the baby was coming.

"Don't be silly," said the QARANC Major. "It'll be ages yet."

I started panting. She ran for a wheelchair and – as I was lifted onto the delivery table – our second son, Tom shot out. By a fortunate feat of dexterity, she caught him. For the rest of my stay she apologized repeatedly for the 'poor delivery'.

Just because I was a new mother there was no let-up in diplomatic duties, and three weeks after the baby's arrival we gave a drinks party at home. I wore a cocktail dress which I considered very flattering. It was in peach-coloured silk with a slightly raised waist and a semi-gathered skirt. I was proudly wearing this when the Turkish Cypriot Minister of Defence came up and patted the front of my skirt.

"Not long now," he grinned.

"Actually, he is three weeks old and upstairs."

I have always been struck by the intense attention given to fertility in the Middle East. In Saudi Arabia, a woman's first question to another is often, "How's your womb?" Even hardened businessmen take an interest. Before Tom, our second child, was born we were dining with the managing director of Olympic Airways (not Aristotle Onassis, who was the owner). He suddenly called down the table to me to "stand up, turn sideways". I did.

"Yes," he announced. "We all think it will be a girl this time."

Although Cyprus really is Aphrodite's isle, complete with frescoed churches, turquoise seas and one of the most hospitable populations in the world, it becomes parochial after two years, which is when the British government pay for leave. Boredom was a problem in such a confined community, but occasionally something cultural happened.

The British Council brought an English ballet company to dance *The Sleeping Beauty* at the open-air Roman theatre at Curium, which is romantically positioned on the Mediterranean coast. This was such an unusual event everyone coveted a ticket, including, we gathered, but could not quite believe, Archbishop Makarios himself. It was a balmy night and the air was full of moisture which became obvious as the dancers slipped and slithered across the stage. The show stopped while the staff did their best to mop the wet stage. We were sitting near the front and during one of these pauses I turned round to see the Archbishop sitting bang in the middle of a row about three behind us.

"He's here," I hissed into Oliver's ear.

"Blow me down."

The ballet continued, only for the lights to go out.

"Watch the Archbishop," muttered Oliver.

When the lights came on again, they revealed the crouching Archbishop trying to creep out along his row. He stood up straight, pretending that he was just looking around, then sat down again.

"He's been really jumpy since his helicopter was shot down," observed Oliver.

It had been drummed into me that maintaining morale was everyone's concern *en poste*. Quite apart from humane considerations about living away from familiar support, there was always the suspicion, in those Cold War days, that the KGB watched for vulnerable individuals who could be blackmailed. During our postings we encountered some sad and largely unexplained personal crises, which sometimes led to repatriation.

In November 1973 after the Ramsbothams had left, Oliver was summoned by the Commander of the Sovereign Base Area to be told that the new High Commissioner's mental condition was an unacceptable security risk and that Oliver, as the most senior member of the High Commission, should make arrangements to send him home. For some time the staff had been aware of strange episodes in the family and it was with a sense of relief that he was repatriated to the Maudsley Hospital in London.

I had a strange experience when Oliver and I dropped in on the Military Attaché and his wife, Gwyneth. They welcomed us in and soon we were enjoying scones with home-made jam. Guy was cleaning his pistol, which was a little unnerving, but I ignored it. Then he raised the gun and pointed it straight at my eyes. For a few moments he and I were locked in a silent sadomasochistic state. Frozen but unflinching, I stared down the barrel wondering about his motive and how to return to the normality of tea and scones. Meanwhile, Oliver and Gwyneth were chatting away, oblivious to the charade being played out under their noses. Silently, Guy lowered the weapon and went back to polishing it. Nobody said anything. They left Cyprus soon after.

Few of the diplomatic wives had paid jobs, as far as I remember, and in those days a wife had to have permission from the Head of Mission if she wanted to work. As wife of the Head of Chancery, I had a particular duty to look after morale, so I floated the idea of a wives' monthly trip to some Cypriot institutions. To my delight this was enthusiastically taken up.

Our first visit was to a towel factory where we all bought excellent quality towels at very little cost. Years later I was in Liberty's in London, and bumped into an important-looking Middle Eastern gentleman whom I vaguely recognised.

"Hello," I said, wondering how I could establish his

provenance. "I know you, but I am afraid I can't remember if you are an Arab or a Greek."

Luckily, he took this in good part. "I'm the owner of the Cypriot towel factory you visited. I am a supplier to this store."

"Gosh, that's impressive."

"Yes, but not surprising. Do you still have your towels?"

"Use them all the time."

"Quality shows, even after ... what is it, 30 years, eh?"

Another visit was to the Presidential Palace. I had suggested this half-jokingly to Archbishop Makarios' secretary and to my surprise, he jumped at the idea. So on the appointed day a group of wives poured out of a bus and wandered freely through the house where Sir Hugh Foot, when Governor of Cyprus, had lived. Although fairly grand it was exceedingly dull. As we toured one olive-green bedroom after another (each furnished with a chenille bedcover) one of the wives announced in a broad Scottish accent: "Simple but tasteful".

After the disappointing tour we were offered refreshments and stood around awkwardly with some of the Archbishop's aides. I suddenly became aware of a stiffening in the atmosphere and thought we had outstayed our welcome. The Archbishop's secretary indicated that the small bald man next to him had something to say. Totally unrecognisable without his hat and gown, there stood Makarios. He said he had just come from the pool, so we had a silly conversation about swimming. A wasted opportunity, but I never thought that he would bother to meet a gaggle of diplomatic wives.

The Cypriot infrastructure was robust and flexible, perhaps resulting from their pragmatism and our colonial legacy. An example of this was the day when for some reason, I was asked to meet our third Military Attaché on his arrival at Nicosia Airport. I had diplomatic status so could walk right up to the aircraft steps. If the Attaché was surprised by the low level of his welcoming party he did not show it; he was a friendly, jovial man. We walked into the Customs Hall. He was carrying a canvas hold-all.

"Excuse me, sir." Our way was barred by a fat, sweaty Customs officer.

"We have diplomatic immunity," I said.

"There is a problem, madam. Excuse me, sir, you are carrying a sword, I believe?"

"Actually, yes. I brought it because of the Presenting Credentials Ceremony tomorrow." He unzipped his bag and produced the weapon in its scabbard.

"One moment, please."

Breathing heavily, the official bustled off into a half-glazed office where we could see him gesticulating. He returned.

"The problem is, sir," he explained politely, "already there is one ceremonial sword registered to the British High Commission. No additional weapon longer than seven inches may be imported while there is another in the country."

The new Military Attaché remained unfazed. He unsheathed his sword and held it gleaming vertically against his nose. "Right. Please bring me some metal cutters so that I can cut this down to seven inches. When I present arms tomorrow and the Archbishop asks why my sword is so short, I'll tell him the reason."

For a moment we stood in silence. Finally, the Customs officer gulped and mopping his brow, looked round to see who might be listening. After a moment he said confidentially, "I think sir, I might make an exception in view of the imminent ceremony."

"Good man! Right decision." As we drove off the Attaché remarked, "What sensible people these Cypriots are."

In 1971 there was a football match between Cyprus and Northern Ireland, and we were asked to organise a reception for the home team. A large crowd got wind of what was happening and gathered outside, hoping to see someone I had never heard of called George Best. George and his teammate, Derek Dougan, noisily entered the house together, cracking jokes and roaring with laughter. I offered them a drink. Rather strangely I thought at the time, although with hindsight I understand why, Derek Dougan said, "No, we're healthy, we are. Have you got any bananas?" I suspect he was already aware of Best's predilection for alcohol.

By chance I had bought a large bunch that day and sent the lads into the kitchen. They sat there and ate quite a few before being ushered to the waiting buses for their next engagement. They signed the Visitors' Book that we kept on the hall table which unfortunately later disintegrated in my parents' flooded basement. So I have no souvenir of that occasion when one of the world's most famous footballers came to my house and ate bananas.

We did have other mementos of our stay, however. There was a thriving undercover trade in ancient pots, and we wanted to buy one or two. Kieran Prendergast, who had met us on arrival in Cyprus, knew exactly which Turk to ask. We drove miles out into the countryside to meet a little old man with a hidden stash. He drove a hard bargain. Having bought two we suffered a crisis of conscience and confessed our illegal purchase to the Director of Antiquities.

A few months later our pots were returned to us from the Nicosia Museum with a note attached, saying that we were free to export them as they held no interest for the archaeologists. We were disappointed that our purchase was so mundane, but felt morally superior to our opposite number in the American Embassy, who carelessly boasted that their outgoing diplomatic bag was regularly stuffed with antiquities, which the Cypriot Customs officials were powerless to open.

We were due to leave Cyprus in July 1973 and at first we thought we might be heading to New York, as Oliver had seen a letter not intended for his eyes. I rushed off to Rustem's bookshop and bought a dog-eared two-volume paperback on the history of America. Oliver pored over it all weekend. Then we were told that we were going back to London.

FRUSTRATIONS WITH
THE FOREIGN OFFICE

"Now that you've had three years' holiday you can take over some of the family responsibilities," were Oliver's sister's words when she met us at the airport. Holiday! But I suppose that is how a posting to Cyprus might seem to people struggling through long, grey English winters.

After months of searching we found a pair of adjoining derelict cottages in the middle of a Hampshire field that eventually became our beloved home for 12 years. (Sadly, we only managed to live in it for four.) The builders worked at a snail's pace to convert our cowmen's cottages into a house while we stayed with my parents for the first year of our two-year stint at home until our patience ran out and we camped in the unfinished structure. Every evening at around 9.30pm, exhausted by the day's activities, including Oliver's commute to London, we forced ourselves to pick up paintbrushes and work until bed time. We resumed this punishing regime – this time turning a field of couch grass into a real garden – after our next foreign posting a few years later.

The house gobbled up all our savings, so we lived frugally. Oliver put up and shot pheasants in the garden before work – the policeman who bred the birds also had to sign Oliver's shotgun licence. To boost our income, Oliver translated Arabic and Turkish texts for the Home Office on the train home.

Many of these were letters written from prison by a young female Palestinian terrorist, which presented a rather different image from her frightening public persona. In these, she appeared as a dutiful daughter whose only concern was the welfare of her family.

At this time Oliver and another official visited Tripoli on the rather thin excuse of a show-jumping competition starring Colonel Harry Llewellyn. Their mission was to persuade the Libyan regime to stop shooting what they called 'stray dogs' (ie, dissidents) in London, and thereby improve relations with Britain. Anticipating a sober Christmas that year we were astonished when a wooden box appeared on the doorstep. Three bottles of vintage champagne from Colonel Gaddafi! In compliance with FCO rules, we gave one away to the Office, but drank to our own very good health on Christmas Day.

After an evening out at the Egyptian Embassy, I discovered that it had cost me £25 for the fare, babysitting and a small present. I wrote to the FCO explaining that our income did not cover my expenses and asked whether they could help those of us who had occasional representational duties at home. The not unexpected reply from Personnel Department ran something like this: "It is always welcome news that spouses continue to support officers on home postings. We hope you will feel able to perform this valuable role in the future ..."

I had been silly to hope for anything different. Then it struck me that I often found myself standing in the Post Office behind some woman drawing her Family Allowance. Didn't the Beveridge Report say it was a universal benefit paid to the mother? That evening I quizzed Oliver. He thought it was paid with his salary.

"I bet it's not. And if it is, it shouldn't be."

He made enquiries. It transpired that diplomatic wives were not receiving Family Allowances. I was so incensed that I sounded off to a friend who, in order to shut me up, said, "If you are that bothered, for goodness sake go and see someone in Personnel."

So that is what I decided to do. Having explained my mission and made an appointment I arrived bang on 11am at the Foreign Office, climbing the familiar stairs to the reception desk where the ladies peered over their half-moon glasses. One, in a gravelly voice, asked my business and then picked up the phone. I was shocked to be told that Mr Masefield had double booked. Could I come back tomorrow?

No, I jolly well could not! I demanded to speak to him. The women exchanged dubious glances but waved me towards a telephone in the adjoining waiting room, an ornate, marble expanse designed by Victorian architects to reflect the magisterial dignity of the Foreign Office. Some dejected-looking people were slumped on the multitude of chairs and sofas. I lifted the telephone receiver. The conversation was amplified many times as it echoed round the lofty chamber.

"Remind me what it is about." I imagined Mr Masefield stifling a yawn.

"You owe me some money; I wrote to you. Don't you remember?"

"Was this about Family Allowances? How much are you arguing about?"

I had no idea. "One thousand pounds," I said. Then added loudly to underline my point, "It's for an abortion."

The slumped figures started into life, craning their heads round pillars and porticos. "I look forward to hearing from you," I said haughtily, replaced the receiver and stomped back to Waterloo Station.

Quite soon afterwards wives on home postings found themselves issued with Family Allowance books.

It was 1975 and we had spent two happy years at home. With two small boys I was in no position to work but I still held fast to my ambition of one day becoming a social worker. The boys had started nursery school and we had all made friends, but we knew we would soon be on the move. Heady thoughts of the world as our oyster were set against considerations of Oliver's career, aging parents and children's education. There were also pressing practical issues. Should I buy winter coats? When should I start to run down the larder? For months I felt constrained by not knowing what surprise the FCO was going to spring. One Friday Oliver arrived home with the tell-tale crimson-covered Post Report in his bag and a hangdog expression on his face.

"Vienna. Not the Embassy, but the United Kingdom Mission to the disarmament conference."

"Great!" I exclaimed, thinking that at least we would be in Europe.

"Do you really think so?" He disappeared mournfully into the loo.

On Monday everything changed. Personnel Department had evidently had a rethink. He bounced in.

"You'll never guess – Political Counsellor, Jeddah! Wonderful news."

He was ecstatic. Not knowing much about Saudi Arabia I was intrigued at the prospect. It presented challenges, as yet mostly unknown. Our arrival was planned for August 1975, just after King Faisal had been killed by his nephew and King Khalid had ascended the throne. So how stable would the regime be? Answer: solid as a rock.

SAUDI ARABIA ARRIVAL AND
A ROYAL ROAD TRIP

When we arrived in Jeddah it was 3am and pitch dark. I stepped from the plane and was knocked backwards by what I thought was heat from the engines. A second later I realised this was Jeddah's night-time temperature. The Administration Officer stood beaming at the foot of the steps and with a magisterial flourish, told his minions that we would go ahead in the car and they could deal with the baggage. We drove off straight into a locked, unmanned barrier, then spent some time zig-zagging backwards and forwards across the tarmac trying to find a way out. This was a compelling metaphor for the next two and a bit years.

In 1975, there was a feeding frenzy in Saudi Arabia. The world's developed countries were vying to benefit financially from the vast oil wealth which had been building up since 1941, when the US began developing the oil fields in the eastern part of the Kingdom. The Americans had established ARAMCO, a company through which oil was produced and traded, and where thousands of US personnel lived and worked. To service the oil industry and build a modern infrastructure, many of the world's poorest nations were supplying cheap labour. It seemed that countries were prepared to do anything to get oil money, and the Saudis certainly exercised their power. Soon after we arrived I wrote home:

Dear Mum and Dad
O is going bonkers trying to arrange Prince Fahd's visit to
GB next week. The Saudis are most concerned that they
will be shown enough respect. A telegram arrived from
London at 3am and O and HE (the Ambassador) zipped
off to Riyadh at 6am to see Prince F. The FCO are doing
their nut having to tell the Queen to change her diary
and Harold (Wilson) and Denis (Healy) both standing on
one leg …

Saudi Arabia was an authoritarian state with an absolute monarchy jealously guarded by the al Saud family. The prevailing ideology was Wahhabi, a strictly puritan form of Islam which, together with Sharia Law, made the Kingdom a difficult place to live because restrictions applied both to the indigenous population and to foreigners. There was no freedom of religion, open political debate, or elections. Capital punishment, stoning and amputation were still practised, alcohol and pork products proscribed, censorship was widespread, women were forbidden to drive or travel unaccompanied, and social life between men and women rigidly controlled. It was difficult to see where change might come from since the ruling Royal family brooked no opposition.

Most people, including expatriates, lived on compounds. The British Embassy compound lay five miles outside Jeddah, its only neighbour a detachment of soldiers living in tents opposite the main gate. Goats roamed the surrounding desert wasteland and acted as rubbish collectors; the Yemeni servants deliberately emptied the dustbins over the wall as there was no such thing as a municipal rubbish collection.

The compound contained the Embassy, the Ambassador's Residence and four detached houses for senior officers nicknamed 'Champagne Alley'. Everyone else was housed in smaller accommodation according to rank. There was an irregularly manned nurse's station and a community room where the TAIF (Thank Allah It's Friday) Club did its drinking. The swimming pool was an essential amenity. The whole area comprised about four acres of cultivated desert and was surrounded by 10-foot high walls. By standing on tiptoe you could just see the Red Sea on the other side.

Miles down the Corniche Road was one of the many Royal palaces and beyond that, the remnants of the old picturesque port of Jeddah. The *suq* and much-extolled fish market were there, too. But because of the restriction on women driving and with no other transport available, I only managed to get to the old part of Jeddah three times in 27 months. And never to the fish market.

"Remember, we are only allowed to take papers and documents with us on the plane," Oliver had said before we left England. "All the toys and clothes have to go in our unaccompanied luggage which will follow afterwards."

"I can't believe it. Who's to know?"

"I'd prefer you to do as the Office says, Julia." I recognised the tiresome "don't try to mess with my employer" voice, and sighed.

So, obediently we arrived in Jeddah with bank statements and insurance documents and very little else. At the last moment I incautiously threw in the grubby contents of the laundry basket and we arrived in the knockout heat of an Arabian August night dressed for autumnal Hampshire.

Oliver had chosen to travel in his new pale-blue cotton suit. A month later he was still wearing it.

"I really must wash it. The pockets are black and it doesn't smell good."

"I don't think that's necessary. It won't be long before our heavy baggage is released."

"Who says?"

"I do. There isn't anything in it that they could possibly object to."

"Humph. Please ask around the Embassy for some clothes.

I've already borrowed stuff for the boys – not that they wear much in this heat."

"And how about you?"

"You know those two long madras cotton dresses I wear all the time? I went to a *thobe* maker with another wife who commandeered the Embassy weekly shopping bus. So I'm OK. But I wish we had some books and toys."

Four months later, the Saudi authorities released our baggage. Meanwhile we lived in an empty, echoing house with the Embassy float of four brown Pyrex plates, cups and saucers, one saucepan and a potato masher. This was a test of ingenuity involving a lot of washing up (particularly of the one saucepan) and the serial cooking of dishes. Because of the climate things did not get cold very quickly, so you could make the bolognese sauce, put it to one side, wash up the saucepan and then boil the spaghetti.

Fortunately, the kids' main entertainment was running around the sweltering compound in a gang of boys (and one girl) all aged about four, so they did not notice the lack of toys. I worried about the extraordinarily long and vicious spines which sprouted at child eyeball level from the end of every cactus plant which grew all over the compound alongside the poisonous oleander. Call me neurotic, but every few weeks I took the kitchen scissors and snipped off every thorn I could find. There was no possibility of taking the children out as mothers do at home, even had there been somewhere to go. We spent most afternoons lounging around the swimming pool. I longed for something to break the silence of our house.

As Political Counsellor Oliver was number three in the Embassy, so we were allocated a 'Champagne Alley' house. The accommodation must have been designed to Saudi specifications because the compound was Saudi owned. But strangely for a country that did not permit men and women to mingle we had only one large, open-plan living room. The kitchen with its windows positioned at ceiling height and no air conditioning ("because that is where the servants work") was the only other room on the ground floor.

Upstairs were four bedrooms and two bathrooms. I was told that the colour schemes of the four big houses had been designed by students at an English art college. We were fortunate in the desert heat to have a cool, pale blue-and-gold theme, which was infinitely preferable to that of our neighbours: they suffered screaming pink and red, with great scarlet circles decorating their sitting-room curtains.

Before we left Britain, the FCO told me to get our GP to ascertain our blood groups. Oliver, as an FCO employee, had been given a medical MOT by St Thomas' Hospital. Our doctor regarded me and the two children gloomily.

"The NHS doesn't really offer that service. But everything I read in the newspapers suggests that the Saudis have state-of-the-art hospitals, so I advise you to get it done out there."

He was half right: the Saudis did have state-of-the-art hospitals, but they were unfortunately devoid of staff. So after a few weeks nagging from the Consul, who wanted to file away our completed medical forms, I requested Embassy transport to a 'highly recommended' downtown laboratory in Jeddah. When the vehicle failed to appear Oliver drove us, which turned out to be extremely fortuitous.

We sat for a while on plastic chairs in a filthy waiting room with a dirty stone floor, and a crooked air conditioner roughly plumbed into a window. Broken Venetian blinds hung at angles over other windows set in the cracked and peeling walls. Then the blood taker emerged in a grimy *thobe* and a crocheted hat. He wiped the syringe he was holding on the skirt of his *thobe*, and accidently dropped it on the floor.

"Please would you fetch me a clean syringe," I said as he bent to pick it up.

"What is wrong with this one?"

"You just dropped it on the floor."

"I don't think so. You may have bad eyesight."

"Oliver," I screamed. He had stepped outside. "Come here and tell him in Arabic that we need clean syringes."

"He's probably a Pakistani and doesn't speak Arabic."

"I don't care, you've got to say something. He won't listen to a woman."

The man gave a sly and compliant smile as he went into the back room to find another, or more likely, just to bring the same implement back. We received confirmation of our blood groups.

About six months later the phone rang in the middle of the night.

"Who is that?" I asked, half asleep.

"Sheikh Mohamed's office."

"It's three in the morning."

"The Sheikh requires a beta positive transfusion."

"And ...?"

"I happen to know Mrs Miles is beta positive ..."

"Have you tried a member of his family?" I said, slamming down the phone.

Bloody cheek! And whatever happened to medical confidentiality?

Our first Ambassador in Jeddah, Alan Rothnie, was a rough diamond. His wife was an aloof blonde who was rumoured not to wear knickers. She also never stayed in post more than three months at a time, which meant that she retained scarcity value and her arrivals generated huge excitement. I first became aware of her presence when a buzz went round a supermarket where I was shopping.

Soon afterwards I was at a wives' coffee morning in the Residence when I introduced her by name to a woman who, I remember, was called Elizabeth Taylor. At once she took hold of the tip of my little finger in a sharp pinch and led me out of the room.

"Never, ever, introduce me that way again," she chided.

I guess it was important to her to be introduced as 'the wife of the British Ambassador,' or perhaps even 'Her Excellency ...' All Heads of Missions take the title 'His Excellency' and are referred to by their staff as 'HE'. Insisting on this protocol in that way did not endear her to me.

Not long after this incident, Mr Rothnie asked us to help out with a diary clash. A tangle of visitors was due to arrive in Jeddah, amongst them Sir Michael Palliser, the Permanent Under-Secretary (PUS) at the Foreign Office, as well as the Duke and Duchess of Gloucester. We were briefly to look after the former and then take over the latter from the Ambassador and accompany them to Dharan, which was located on the Persian Gulf. We were fairly new in post and someone who knew my views on Saudi Arabia advised:

"Don't say anything negative to the PUS. Keep your trap shut."

We invited Sir Michael to tea. He was white-haired, handsome, patrician and, I felt, inscrutable. I rustled up cucumber sandwiches with home-made brown bread for which he seemed rather grateful. The conversation was desultory until he suddenly sank back into his armchair and gripped his forehead.

"What a hellhole," he said.

"Would you mind saying that again in case I misheard you," I asked, astonished.

"What a hellhole," he obligingly repeated.

The next day and with huge reluctance I left my two little boys in the care of another wife and drove with Oliver to the airport to join the Duke and Duchess of Gloucester. It was the first time I had ever been parted from the children and though fretting, I felt I had to do my duty. We rendezvoused with the Ambassador and his wife, who had spent the previous day with the Royal party and were looking rather strained. All Mrs Rothnie could say to me through gritted teeth was: "Drink gin".

We were introduced to Lieutenant Colonel Simon Bland, a jovial but stressed aide to their Royal Highnesses. The Gloucesters were trailblazing for HM the Queen (who later paid a very successful visit to Saudi Arabia) but they were an idiosyncratic couple with ideas of their own. The Embassy had sent specific dress instructions which they had ignored, and I was told later that the Duchess came down the aircraft steps in hat, high heels, tights and a skirt that had to be grasped tightly to prevent the street urchins looking up it as it billowed in the wind. Throughout the visit I, complying with Saudi requirements, was wearing sandals and one of my two madras check-cotton ankle-length *thobes*.

Simon told us we would be travelling in an aircraft of the Queen's Flight, sitting with the Royal couple. I knew it was their young son's second birthday that day so I had brought a Maria Theresa dollar (which, because of its standard silver content , had previously been Saudi currency), all wrapped up for them to give him as a memento of his parents' visit.

We entered the four-seater cabin where the Royals were installed face-to-face across a table. I knew I was not supposed to address them unless they acknowledged me. They did not. They also ignored the Rothnies, whom I could see feverishly waving goodbye on the steaming tarmac. I kept putting my hand inside my *thobe* pocket fingering the dollar and wondering what to do. Since not one word passed between us during the entire flight, I still have it.

We stopped to refuel. Back on terra firma the Air Marshall asked whether we would like to move to another part of the aircraft. We exchanged places with him and Simon, and thoroughly enjoyed the treat of a Devon cream tea high above the desert, chatting to a Dickensian detective and a Lady-in-Waiting who was suffering from laryngitis and lost her voice for the remainder of the visit.

We landed first in Taif where the Duke, an architect, visited his old tutor Sir Leslie Martin, who was building the new Saudi government complex there. We were accompanied by Algie Asprey, who – on the strength of running an exclusive Bond Street emporium – was retained as the Saudi Royal interior decorator. I took the Duchess on a tour of the *suq*. It was uncomfortably hot and she seemed out of sorts, but agreed to visit the silver *suq* where men were hammering lumps of silver into beads for necklaces.

"That's not silver," she said. She did not want to see carpets so we cut the visit short.

That evening we were bidden to dine with the Danish Ambassador, Oliver's old friend from Jordan. I sat on his left. The Duchess, who is Danish by birth, sat on his right and as protocol decreed, for the first two courses he concentrated on conversation with her. As the pudding arrived he turned to me, pulling a face that told it all. I comforted myself that it was not only I who found the Duchess difficult.

In the Eastern Province we visited the impressive Petromin University, set high on a hill overlooking the American ARAMCO estate with its lofty air- conditioned halls, fountains and vast, carpeted library. That evening there was an informal supper and for almost the first time the Duke spoke to me.

"I see you're wearing your nightie again."

Prissily I replied: "It's the custom here not to show your legs in public. In Jeddah, the Religious Police slap green paint on any exposed female flesh. I have a friend who reads the radio news here and has to cover her wrists while on air, even though nobody can see her."

He turned away, seized a bread roll and with a lot of guffawing, stuffed it down Simon Bland's shirt. They left the following day.

It was not only British Royalty that we met; I also had contact with Saudi Royalty and wrote home:

Dear Mum and Dad
Princess Johara gave an evening garden party in her Jeddah bungalow. If you had all the money in the world where would you build your house? Hers is the first house at the end of the airport runway. She's evidently keen on planes as she's done the same in Riyadh. The Princess is the second of three wives of King Feisal. She looks like a fat, dark gypsy – ugly and shapeless with long straight black hair and very red lips. She was lying asleep on a bench when we arrived. She has two daughters by two husbands, the younger has learning difficulties. They were both at the party …

When the Ambassador and his wife were leaving Jeddah, we offered to give a farewell dinner, and as is customary, they gave us a suggested guest list. This included some Saudi names. Knowing how unreliable Saudis were, I made Oliver phone each of the guests every week to remind them of this important occasion. On the day of the dinner Oliver rang round again. One man – let's call him Mohamed Ali – replied:

"I'm sorry, I won't be able to come as my wife is in labour. And I always visit my mother on Wednesdays."

Oliver, not a little riled, retorted: "But surely you knew about this before?"

"Yes of course I did, but you never asked. I will make every effort to come."

Assuming he would not, I removed a place setting and sat down with the Ambassador and Mrs Rothnie to await their guests. One was from the Ministry of Foreign Affairs and by a process of elimination I decided it was Mohamed Ali. So I was a bit surprised when the door opened and the Ambassador said to Oliver in an audible whisper:

"Whoever's that? Not one of mine."

We welcomed him in and as unobtrusively as possible in our open-plan living room, I re-laid the place setting. At dinner, I sat next to him.

"So you are from the Ministry of Foreign Affairs," I began.

"I am afraid you are mistaken, madam," he replied courteously.

"But you know the Ambassador?"

"No. It is a great pleasure to meet him." I was non-plussed.

Finally, "I'm the government meteorologist," he said.

The mystery was solved when we discovered that Oliver had indeed been phoning the Mohamed Ali of the Ministry of Foreign Affairs except for the final call when he had mistakenly got hold of a telephone number for the meteorologist with the same name. Typically, and in the circumstances, fortunately, the Ministry of Foreign Affairs man had not bothered to show up. Atypically, the meteorologist had responded very positively to the last-minute invitation.

Quite soon after this dinner party we left for home leave after 18 unbroken months in post. I sat down in my allocated British Airways seat next to a rather good-looking Arab dressed in a dark suit and silk tie.

"Hello." He shocked me.

"Sorry, but do I know you?"

"Yes, of course you do – I am the man you thought came from the Ministry of Foreign Affairs. Remember?" He grinned. "Tell me – why did you ask me to that party for your Ambassador?"

A year later, he again hailed me in a friendly fashion. This time he was wearing tennis whites, so again I failed to recognise him. All these outfits made fertile ground for social gaffes.

NEW SKILLS AND
OLD STRUGGLES

"Oh no, don't tell me they're going to let us down," I heard a woman say. One was crying. Another, who had gone into the Office to enquire, reappeared. "The trip's off, girls," she said.

A group of wives had hatched a plan to circumvent the lack of transport. Although the Embassy was supposed to have a complement of six cars, it rarely rose above three because of the attrition rate on the roads. The wives had thought that if they all went into town on the same morning, they could book an Embassy car that would drop each of them off and then go round picking them up again. I happened to be passing as the group assembled outside the Embassy. On my return trip they were still waiting.

"Look," I said, "the Ambassador's Austin Princess is standing right there. Get in and go. I'll tell him what's happened. He never gets up much before 10.00 anyway."

They sailed off in air-conditioned comfort and I squared it with the Ambassador, who took it like a lamb. I felt it was important to assert the wives' rights as our needs were invariably overridden by other considerations. The prohibition on women driving had far-reaching consequences. Oliver pointed out that it had a negative impact on men's lives, too, although he managed to maintain his umblemished record of shopping avoidance even in Saudi Arabia. However, for an extended period he did drive the Embassy children to school each time the Office transport let us down.

I knew that if an opportunity to drive presented itself I would be unable to resist. Passing my test six years earlier had been one of the most liberating experiences of my life. Here, the second-hand car we had bought from our predecessor was mostly redundant except as an adjunct to the oven. It was possible to warm plates and make meringues (when we could get eggs) on the scalding hot roof. Not being free to travel around was an insult as well as an obstacle.

With a daily accident rate 30 times as high in Jeddah as the annual rate in the UK, it was unusual to be on the road without seeing an accident or its aftermath. Unsurprisingly, we had friends who had been injured or killed, including the Greek Ambassador. The accident rate was sky high because there were no traffic lights, Highway Code, or driving test and the Saudis drove as if they were riding camels. I saw children being lifted up into the driving cab of large, sometimes articulated, lorries and watched, horrified, as they manoeuvred them out into the traffic. Smoking was commonplace at petrol stations. I once noticed a man, lit cigarette in mouth, remove a manhole cover and peer down into the open underground tank before the fuel lorry decanted its load. My driver laughed when I asked him to move away fast.

Embassy staff were warned never to stop at the scene of an accident. If we did we risked taking the blame and having to pay blood money. In 1975, this was about £26,000 for a Saudi and less for everyone else. Until a culprit had been identified the body would remain untouched. I witnessed this when a putrid smell wafted into our house and I realised that the smashed lorry left for four days in the heat on the other side of our wall contained the driver's rotting corpse.

Every day, I and Anita Michael, who also had a young child, went with Embassy transport to collect our children from playgroup. But one glorious day a row of drivers sat immobile on a low wall at our normal meeting place. They grinned and waved but made no move.

"Mohamed, we have to go – we'll be late."

"Mr Herdman, no sign." Mohamed made a scribbling gesture in the air. For the first half of our time in Jeddah, Mark Herdman, the Head of Chancery, was responsible for authorising transport.

"Well, never mind that. You know we go every day."

He refused to budge. Anita and I conferred. "I can't ask Oliver to take us as he's got a slipped disc and is lying on the floor."

"Alan's away, I'm afraid."

"There's only one thing for it, then. We'll have to drive. What do you think?"

"They always leave the car key in the lock."

We jumped into the Land Cruiser and I switched on the ignition. After months of incarceration, liberation swept over me. We drove out of the gates and round the block. "I'll go back and see if I've shaken them up," I said.

The drivers had not moved. They just waved a bit more and one shouted, "Right drive, right drive."

"I think he means drive on the right," Anita said.

I had a sudden, ghastly thought. "Oh no, I have no idea where to go. I've never concentrated on the route as I never thought I'd have to drive."

"I think I know." She was wonderfully calm.

We arrived at school a little shaken, but rather pleased with ourselves. I could not resist saying nonchalantly, "Anita and I drove here today."

"You never!"

"You watch." As I pulled away I looked in the rear mirror and saw a line of open-mouthed Europeans standing in the road.

We reached the Embassy compound safely. The phone rang. It was Mark Herdman's secretary. "Mr Herdman wonders if you could pop over to his office for a few minutes." I was expecting this.

Mark, and his wife Betsy, were good friends of ours. He greeted me with a broad grin. "You know what I have to say, don't you?"

"That I have been very naughty and must never do it again."

"Seriously, Julia, if you had knocked down a Saudi you would be looking at a huge sum in blood money. It just wouldn't be funny. And it wouldn't be good for Oliver's career, either."

"Today was just ridiculous. The drivers wouldn't go because they hadn't received their orders. I wouldn't have done it if children hadn't been involved."

"OK. Let's call it quits."

Years later Brian Lees, the Military Attaché, said to me: "I arrived at the airport that day and everyone was talking about your escapade. You brought the whole of Jeddah to a standstill."

On the day our second Ambassador, John Wilton, was arriving with his wife Maureen, we all smartened up – as much as was possible in cotton *thobes* – and went to greet them at Jeddah Airport. Mark and Betsy Herdman could hardly contain themselves. Their daughter Deirdre was arriving for the Easter holidays on the same flight, after her first term at boarding school. They were anxious that their absence from the welcoming party might be noticed.

"Don't be daft. You concentrate on Deirdre," everyone told them.

The plane landed and we all stood to attention. After a long delay one of the cabin crew came down the steps to identify the British Consul, who immediately went on board. A British national had died during the flight. Passengers started emerging and the Herdmans nipped towards steerage. We gathered round our new chief and his wife, assessing their potential.

Someone muttered, "Red hair – always a danger sign."

"And she's bringing a Pekinese, in this climate! I ask you …"

We made to move off when I saw Betsy and Mark frantically running around. "She's not on the plane," Betsy gasped, close to tears. "Mark's trying to phone the school. But you go and look after HE."

Back at the compound I knocked on the Herdmans' door. "Any news?"

"You will never believe what happened. Deirdre told the headmistress she was flying from Heathrow, but the bus went to Gatwick and she was left all alone not knowing what to do. A BA ground staff person got her to her grandparents, and she'll fly out tomorrow."

"What a nightmare. I dread my turn."

Dear Mum and Dad
I gave a successful tea party for Mrs Wilton to meet some Saudi ladies. Everyone came in their Balenciagas and it turned into a bun-fight. No one ate much. Next time, everything will be in bite-sized pieces. We ladies had an argument as to where the East was as one woman wanted to pray. I am afraid we got it wrong …

One of my irritations with our second Ambassador in Jeddah was that he invariably made Oliver work on Fridays, the Muslim weekend, and our only day off each week. However angry I became, Oliver always meekly assented when he got the early-morning Friday phone call.

The Ambassador and his wife were intent on spending Fridays at the seaside. Jeddah Creek was not an unmitigated blessing. It was by anyone's standards a grotty bit of shoreline. Only the strongest swimmers would venture far out, away from the floating Elastoplast and plastic bottles, to snorkel on the coral reef, returning with impressive tales of exotically coloured fish and occasional sightings of small sharks. But bathers had to wear shoes because of the deadly stone fish lurking in the water. Their long spiny tail could whip your leg if trodden on, injecting poison that would kill in less than an hour.

British expatriates became so anxious about this that the Consul was prevailed upon to "do something". What he could do, when the Creek lay an hour's drive from Jeddah, was anyone's guess, but to get the crowd off his back he succeeded in getting some serum from the Australian Embassy (because the Australians know all about stone fish). There remained the tricky question as to who might administer this stuff, which had to be stored under lock and key in a safe cold place.

A request went out for volunteers. I was an obvious candidate as I was invariably at home on the compound. In the end, six of us got together for a lesson from a nurse. She brought a syringe, a jug of water and an orange. Each of us learned how to draw water up the syringe without creating bubbles, plunge it deftly through the orange rind, and release it. At this point a male diplomat walked out saying "it's all too much".

The rest of us continued to pass the orange round. It became bigger than a grapefruit and considerably heavier with all the water. As it reached football proportions the whole thing exploded, showering us with water, pith and flesh. We all agreed we would never have the courage to inject the real stuff into a live patient on the verge of death. Fortunately, we never had to.

So every Friday while everyone else was disporting themselves at the Creek, the children and I would be left hanging around the empty compound just like any other day of the week, with nothing to do and nowhere to go.

"What can I do?" Oliver would wheedle. "Someone has to look after the shop."

"But why is it always you?"

Trouble in Jeddah usually flared up on Thursday night, which was comparable to Saturday night in Western countries. Every week we would hear of somebody's death, arrest or terrible injury. Oliver was not the Consul but there was a need for a senior diplomat with fluent Arabic to sort out these often self-inflicted events, usually fuelled by the home-made hooch called *siddiqi*, Arabic for 'my friend'.

"An Australian put a meat cleaver in a Brit's head last night. They want to get him home on the afternoon flight and I've got to negotiate with the airline to make room for the stretcher and ensure his passport is in order and everything ..." Late that afternoon he returned.

"You look a bit grey. Did he get on the flight?"

"Oh yes, he's off and away. But they called me to the hospital."

"What on earth for?"

"Well, someone had to give him blood."

"I don't believe it! Literally blood, sweat and tears. What else can the blasted Office ask for?"

He didn't smile. "They took the syringe out of a kidney dish that had lots of cigarette stubs in it."

I thought about hepatitis and seethed.

When I became pregnant in Saudi Arabia, I wondered if I had been irresponsible and foolish. Fortunately, the other wives were encouraging.

"If you're worried, wrap the baby in aluminium foil and hop on the next plane home."

"But there are only three flights a week," I observed grimly.

I was haunted by a tragedy that was ending just as we arrived in post. A young Embassy couple had given birth to a stillborn child. They were presented with a stark choice: either bury him immediately as Arab custom decrees, or keep the tiny corpse in their domestic fridge until they returned home. Nobody seemed to have the wit or imagination to think up a less grotesque solution. It reinforced my view of the heartlessness of the Foreign Office.

The day before my due date was a Friday. Since it was the weekend Oliver had a treat for us: the film of *It Shouldn't Happen to a Vet*. The kids soon got bored but I watched avidly as James Herriot's hero put his arm up a cow's backside and brought out a calf.

"Well, if that doesn't bring it on, nothing will," declared my beloved.

A few hours later he found himself standing at the reception desk of the Saudi Military Hospital. He was able to persuade them that I was yet again a non-entitled civilian, meaning we did not have to pay up front in cash. Prince Sultan, the Minister of Defence, had granted him this unexpected favour. A young, red-haired Irish midwife came up.

"Pop on the trolley, then."

"I'd like Oliver to stay, please."

"Well, that might present a bit of a problem since this is the women's side of the hospital and men are not allowed."

In the meantime, Oliver was pacing the corridor where he met an Arab male doctor smoking a cigarette. "No men." He waved a forefinger in Oliver's face. "You understand? *Verboten*."

Oliver indicated the large neon sign hanging from the ceiling. "You mean 'forbidden' like smoking?" The Arab took the point and Oliver stayed, although there was no room for him in the drugs cupboard where Hugh was born.

Our third son lay incongruously like a large blond whale in the middle of a nursery full of tiny, dark-haired Saudi babies. I contemplated olives and yoghurt for breakfast. An Arab girl loomed up to my bedside halfway through the morning.

"Can I get you to do an exercise for me, please?"

"What do you want me to do?"

"Stay lying on your back. Now, can you clap your hands above your head?"

If this was Saudi physiotherapy I quite liked it and obediently flapped and clapped.

"I'm a trainee nurse and I have to get someone to do it. None of the women in here will move for 40 days after giving birth, so I'm very grateful to you."

She must have been one of the first cohorts of Saudi student nurses. Their training was delivered remotely by phone and TV, as there were few professional women to teach them and direct contact with Saudi men was forbidden. She refused to answer when I asked if she nursed male patients.

At the age of 31, I was the oldest and largest in that maternity ward. As it was a military hospital, most of the girls were teenagers married to Saudi soldiers. The girl in the bed opposite me was aged 14, and having her second child. She had lost her first in childbirth because her hips were too narrow. When she combed her hair she drew the curtains round her bed and then having veiled her head walked down the ward naked, her hennaed hands and feet showing that she had recently attended a wedding or some other celebration.

The Duke of Edinburgh visited Riyadh, Saudi Arabia's capital city. I felt I couldn't present myself in the same old *thobe* the Duke of Gloucester had commented on, so since it was a British Royal occasion, I decided to wear a summer dress with tights (because I assumed that Royalty could not be exposed to bare legs), despite still being overweight after childbirth.

As the Embassy party waited at the airport for the Duke's arrival, the wives became aware of the need for a loo but naturally there wasn't one for women. It became super urgent for me because I felt my tights, stretched to their utmost elasticity, creeping steadily down my thighs until they came to rest around my knees, threatening to appear below my hemline. We lined up as the Royal plane came into view. The door opened and the Saudi silver band struck up tuneless renditions of the two National Anthems.

"Nothing to do with us, Sir," commented the Ambassador as the Duke winced at the cacophony.

The Duke walked first along the line of Saudi dignitaries and then the British. I was wondering how I was going to curtsey with my tights round my knees but the Duke did not bother to do more than grunt in my direction and suddenly all the men vanished, leaving the four British diplomats' wives standing in the broiling sun. We tried one gate after another but discovered we were ignominiously locked in.

"I can't get over that fence – my knees are locked together."

"I don't know why you ever thought of wearing those stupid tights.

"There's only one thing for it," remarked the Ambassador's wife, eyeing a negligible gap in the chicken-wire fence. A passing Saudi policeman in a pancake beret could hardly believe his eyes as four sweaty, puffing British ladies eased themselves through it. A few minutes later we were back in air conditioning. But there was no loo, because women do not count.

> Dear Mum and Dad
> Prince Fahd invited the men, including the Duke, to a banquet at his palace. When O came home we all wanted to know what he'd had to eat. "Nothing," he said morosely. The Saudis had not arranged for an interpreter or the one appointed got cold feet – so they asked O to do it. When he got to the top table there was no chair and feeling conspicuous, he knelt on the floor between the Duke and Prince Fahd. Eventually someone did bring a chair but eight courses went past, plus tomato ketchup, none of which was offered to O. The Duke's equerry said the food was inedible anyway ...

The next day Oliver and I went to a small lunch with the Duke at one of the King's palaces. Algie Asprey, whom we had met with the Gloucesters, had decorated it in green (a colour favoured by Arabs because of its scarcity in their natural environment). I was so terrified of making a *faux pas* that I barely noticed my surroundings. The overall impression was one of brightness and glitter, lots of huge gilded mirrors and chandeliers and deep-pile bordered carpets that made me feel as if I was sinking in up to my ankles. And of course it was deliciously cool to step into the air-conditioned interior.

I sat next to the Duke but our conversation never got going; he seemed captivated by the lady on his right. I understood that he was not amused at the Saudi convoy he was being carried around in. We had often seen these: a line of scarlet Land Rovers about two feet apart sandwiching a VIP vehicle, racing through the streets at roughly 100 miles per hour. Sad to say, a few weeks after the Duke left, the predicted tragedy occurred when all the vehicles in the convoy concertinaed into one another.

My letter home continued:

That afternoon Oliver had to interpret again at the races and Prince Abdullah – who has a terrible stutter and is hell to translate for – gave him a big bronze medal. The Duke got a gold one. The Duke was also presented with a solid gold statuette of a camel. "Just doubled the gold reserves," he remarked as he pocketed it. And later when he received a watch, he studied it in silence, then said, "Wouldn't be bad if you picked off the diamonds."

At the end of the visit Prince Fahd gave all the Embassy men mishlas (cloaks with gold braid), and headdresses, and either cufflinks or a pen and pencil set. O got cufflinks. HE's wife got a gold watch that she says she'll keep although strictly she is not allowed to. The Duke gave HE some cufflinks with entwined initials and a coronet, and O got a signed photo. Yesterday, HE was bemoaning the fact that he hadn't been given a photo. I didn't mention ours but O was chuffed that the Duke hadn't just handed them out with the rations.

The Duke asked O if he had had anything to eat at the banquet, and O said, "not a sausage". As he was saying goodbye at the airport, the Duke turned to the deputy Chief of Protocol – who was supposed to have done the interpreting – and wagged a finger at him. "You are the one who should have been doing the work," he said. I think the visit was a success and O was involved in all sorts of Royal activities, which he enjoyed …

Beneath the Veil and Entertaining Unpredictably

The rather sweaty-looking mayor of Jeddah came to dinner, albeit without replying to our invitation. He sucked on a fat cigar all the while shovelling food into the other side of his mouth. Having eaten well, he stood up while we were still finishing the pudding.

"I shall have to go; I am invited to dinner tonight," he explained apologetically.

But our diplomatic efforts had been worthwhile. An agreement was made during dinner for a British company to supply dustbins to Jeddah Municipality, although it was still unclear where the contents would be dumped.

When we first arrived in Jeddah we had been told it would be difficult to meet Saudis, although a handful were known to some Embassy colleagues.

"I'm not prepared to stay in a place where I never meet any local people," I told Oliver. But I had no idea how I might achieve it.

"You have to go to a wedding," Caroline Lees, the Military Attaché's wife, said. "It doesn't matter whose. Next time I get an invitation, I'll let you know."

Saudi weddings are three-day events, but the climax comes at about 4am on the final morning when the bride and groom (the only man present, and looking sheepish), parade through a crowd of appraising, ululating women whose shouted comments roughly translate as "Get yer kit off".

Caroline, having a military driver, took me to my first wedding, which familiarised the ritual. Thereafter, whenever I got wind of a wedding I would hitch a lift in the last vehicle leaving the Embassy, which would drop me at about midnight somewhere unknown in Jeddah.

I would then have a three-hour solitary wait amongst rows of hard chairs set out under the stars on an anonymous concrete patch. Once a servant took pity on me and gave me a cardamom seed to chew. I was always worried about how I would get home, but by dawn I had usually made a new Saudi friend who was able to provide a lift, although once it was with someone's 10-year-old son, who had just been given his first Cadillac.

Gradually the wedding concourse would fill up, each woman removing an indistinguishable black *abiyah* to reveal a dazzling designer gown laden with jewels. Before the first wedding, the English wife of a Saudi architect had looked me over and said: "You look fine, but you need to wear all your jewels."

I indicated my earrings and engagement ring. "These are all my jewels."

The women were fascinating. Many evidently had eating disorders as they were painfully thin. Some were wild, shouting in a most unladylike manner. I even witnessed a fight, with chairs being thrown round the concourse, and once I saw an overtly lesbian couple. I had little doubt that their unnaturally restricted lives had a real impact on their psychological health.

At about 5am we would be bidden to the feast, which had been lying out all night in the suffocating heat, so I usually avoided the prawns. I once stood in line behind a guest who took a bite out of each item and carefully replaced it on the serving plate. Having survived the terrifying ride home, I would tiptoe into the bedroom, shoes in hand, as other people were getting up. The exhilaration of going out by myself outweighed any tiredness the next day.

Although I came into contact with many Saudi women at these weddings there was no way to pursue friendships; their lives were so enclosed that it felt intrusive to ask for telephone numbers. But I was determined not to leave Saudi Arabia without getting to know a few of them. I had a stroke of luck. The Danish Ambassador invited us to dinner again. Most Danish diplomats are, in my experience, eccentric so it was hardly surprising that we ate supper sitting at a table fashioned from a fairground carousel. As we milled around beforehand I heard a deep voice speaking good English and turned round expecting to see a man. A Saudi woman was talking in an extraordinary baritone. She wore a long white dress and was smothered in square-cut emeralds.

I didn't know what to say except "What a fabulous necklace."

Immediately friendly, she replied, "Let me tell you how I got it. I was in the *suq* when two women came into the jeweller's shop trying to sell it. I suppose it was an unwanted gift. He made them a ridiculous offer which I doubled and they were happy to accept. It was an absolute bargain."

Mansoura's husband was a Saudi diplomat and they had served in The Hague, which explained her poise and fluent English. We saw each other from time to time and she took me to a wedding.

Dear Mum and Dad
At the wedding we sat with Mansoura's cousin, who was married at 17, and her two younger sisters. The fashions were incredible, ranging from Hijaz traditional costumes – high, white-starched lace collars on long-sleeved pale-coloured dresses and white headdresses that made them look like nuns – right up to Dior and Givenchy, topped off with exotic hairstyles and heavy make-up. The ceremony was held in a garden with carpets on the ground and sofas all around. There were about 200 women. I talked to a French governess who'd just left the job of teaching King Hassan of Morocco's children in order to work for a Saudi business family who only live here about 4-6 months of

the year, spending the rest of the time in London and Paris. She said she had been in the country since January and I was the first non-Arab she'd met.

We had arrived at 10.30pm and at 3.30am I said I'd better leave but the grandmother – younger than me! – who had organised the wedding said I must eat before going and she would get everyone else to eat at the same time. All 200 guests! I insisted that she didn't disturb everyone for my sake, so Mansoura and I were ushered out the back where there was a table measuring about 40 foot, groaning with food. Afterwards I got driven home by one of the chauffeurs at breakneck speed through deserted Jeddah ...

The Foreign Secretary, David Owen, and his wife, Debbie, visited Jeddah on official business, and the Commercial Counsellor's wife, Shirley Kay, and I were instructed to take Mrs Owen to visit Princess Saud, the wife of the Saudi Foreign Minister.

Oliver said, "This is the opportunity you've been waiting for – tell the Princess how difficult it is for wives – and consequently husbands – not being allowed to drive."

In the car we gave Mrs Owen some pointers to protocol in the Kingdom. One thing we emphasised was that the signal for the visit being over was when servants brought out clay pots of burning incense, which we were expected to waft up our skirts.

Princess Saud turned out to be a sad sylph whose world was defined by four walls and her children. Like most Saudi women her spirit had been extinguished long ago by the system and although she was polite and spoke good English there was little in common between her and Mrs Owen, an American and a successful literary agent. All we could do was admire the house and talk superficialities. I expected my plea to the Princess about the driving ban to fall on deaf ears but I was surprised when she responded, "Oh I thought Western women did drive here".

After tea, the incense burners were produced but Mrs Owen made no move to leave. I felt it was not my place to tell her.

The Princess said, "Perhaps you would like to see over the rest of the house?"

Even that hint was insufficient as Mrs Owen leapt up saying, "And perhaps I can meet the children?"

"The children will be going to bed."

At every turn of the staircase there was another servant with an incense burner. Finally I burst out, "I think we really should be going."

When we got outside there was, as usual, no Embassy car. We stood for a while on the litter-strewn street while I pondered what to do. We were just ushering a bemused Mrs Owen into the front seat of a builder's pick-up truck when our driver arrived.

Saudi Arabia in 1976 was the world's honeypot and the Embassy fielded a constant stream of high-level visitors. I described an incident from the British Prime Minister's visit in a letter home:

Dear Mum and Dad
O was away at the beginning of the week with Jim Callaghan in Riyadh. All went well and Jim was jovial and relaxed. On the first night I gather there were high jinks, with Jim saying he was going to bed and then reappearing incognito dressed as an Arab in robes, which gave the Ambassador a bit of a turn as he thought he had been caught in flagrante with a bottle of whisky ...

On another occasion Oliver asked me: "Would you like to meet George Thomas, Speaker of the House of Commons?"

"That sounds interesting."

"Don't get excited, it's only a courtesy visit while he waits at the airport. I think he's with a banker called Hodge. They're off to stay with the Saudi oil minister Sheikh Yamani."

We found them in the VIP lounge and were surprised to find Mrs Thomas there, too. A motherly woman, she confided that they really should be on holiday in Jersey. Speaker Thomas was chatty. Sir Julian Hodge looked preoccupied, perhaps because he was drinking locally made Pepsi Cola. (We had stopped buying the stuff after I found a toothbrush inside the bottle I was drinking.)

"I'm really looking forward to this adventure," Speaker Thomas said in his Welsh lilt. "I didn't know what to give the Sheikh as I imagine he has most things." He produced from his luggage a miner's lamp. "I thought it would be suitable, see, because he's Minister of Energy. Am I correct?"

"Yes," Oliver replied laughing. "It's a lovely present. But I'm more concerned about what they give you in return."

"Oh, that had never occurred to me. What might that be?"

"Well, recently a member of the Royal family was presented with a thoroughbred race horse. That gave the Embassy a bit of a headache."

"I can imagine. So what did you do?"

"We shipped it to Hungary to be quarantined in case it had African horse disease, before it entered Britain."

"My goodness. What a business," he sympathised. "I can't imagine we'll be given anything like that."

He received a couple of Alsatians.

It was nearly impossible to obtain a visitor's visa to the Kingdom but Freddie Beeston, the Professor of Arabic at Oxford and Oliver's one-time tutor, managed to visit. We went together to the *suq* as he wanted to buy a pearl necklace. Freddie cut an extraordinary figure, rather like Old Father Time, with his long white nicotine-stained hair streaming out behind him in the wind. I hoped the religious police wouldn't bop him on the head as they customarily did to anyone who attracted their attention. The male shop assistants stared as Freddie adorned himself with 20 ropes of pearls, finally choosing a couple of strands the colour of his hair. He led a bizarre private life so goodness knows where the pearls were destined.

In our second year in Jeddah, just before we went on leave, I had a brainwave.

"I know how to meet Saudi women," I told Oliver. "I'll hold a Tuesday *soirée* with open house. I'll put on an entertainment and give them supper."

"Before you do anything you'd better square it with HE's wife and ask if she would like to host it."

I made an appointment to see Maureen and explained my idea. She was sitting in the drawing room where numerous flies were buzzing around the panting Pekinese, which was comfortably installed on a fine upholstered armchair. I wondered what the Ministry of Works might have said, had they known.

"My dear girl, if that's what you want to do, just go ahead."

"Would you like to have a standing invitation?"

"I should think that would be fine. You just go on leave and we'll see what happens when you come back." She waved me away like one of the annoying flies.

The Head of Mission's wife can make an enormous difference to a post. I think I hit on two pretty difficult ones in Jeddah. Or perhaps they disliked the place as much as I did, without admitting it.

As soon as we returned I started working on my plan, which was not without complications. Apart from Mansoura I did not know any Saudi women except for Shirley and Caroline's contacts. I had no way of advertising and there was no such thing as a telephone book, even were I able to read it. Finding people who could offer interesting entertainment was also difficult since I was confined to a compound five miles outside Jeddah with no transport. Food was always a problem and unpredictable numbers were going to make things even trickier.

At my first *soirée* Shirley showed some slides and talked about rural England to a small female Arab audience. I asked them to bring their Saudi women friends. The following Tuesday there were probably a dozen Saudi girls present. Most spoke sufficiently good English or could translate, so they all understood that week's talk. The woman speaker described delivering Spitfires from the factory to the frontline during the war for the Air Transport Auxiliary. I admit to deliberately trying to widen Saudi women's horizons.

The women dressed casually in Western clothes under their concealing *abiyah* so jeans and trousers were commonplace, although probably of designer quality. An acknowledged benefit of wearing the veil, as an Arab woman once pointed out to me, is that nobody knows if you're wearing pyjamas underneath, or had neglected to brush your hair. The overriding objective was never to show your legs, so skirts were always floor length. A few inexpensive clothes such as cotton kaftans could be bought in the *suq* but all the stallholders were men, so trying things on was out of the question. One of the ways Saudi women occupied themselves was to get their menfolk to take them to London or Paris for shopping trips, since no female could travel anywhere without a male escort.

Since we only had one reception room, there was an unexpected bonus: Oliver found himself confined to the kitchen with an assortment of men who had brought the women by car. Some of these, husbands or brothers, turned out to be useful contacts whom he would never have met anywhere else. They were forbidden to approach unveiled women so they had to contain their impatience in the stuffy, un-airconditioned space until all faces were covered. I suppose the occasional availability of alcohol in our house was an attraction, as the men did not seem to mind returning.

My idea took off and every Tuesday more women came because, as I had surmised, they were as bored as me. Visiting the British Embassy probably held some fascination, if not kudos.

One day when I was lazing by the swimming pool Petronella, the Security Officer's wife, introduced me to her daughters who were professional ballet dancers. They admitted that they were bored, too.

An idea struck me. "Petronella, would you mind if I asked your daughters to dance for my next Tuesday *soirée*?"

"I've no objection. But where are they going to do this?"

"The only flat space is the concrete dustbin patch outside my front door."

"No points then. I'm not risking them breaking an ankle."

I sent out messages far and wide and on that designated Tuesday got someone to rig up a light that sent a strong beam onto the concrete patch. I found some chairs to make an auditorium and Jaki, our mother's help, and I decided on a menu of lasagne, salad and ice cream with hot chocolate sauce.

At 4pm Oliver phoned to say that a queue had formed round the Embassy with people asking for tickets for that night's performance. I asked Jaki to double the quantity of food. Then he rang again to say that the Saudi Ministry of the Interior had phoned to check whether the girls' legs were going to be exposed.

"Of course – it's ballet. Anyway, how do they even know about it?"

"Everyone knows everything in this country."

"I've got this nice piece of chiffon," Petronella said, producing a whisper of translucent cloth. "They can tuck it in their waistbands and nobody will be able to see their legs – well, sort of." We laughed.

Soon, beautifully groomed women started filling the seats and jewels sparkled everywhere. There was a buzz of anticipation. Maureen, the Ambassador's wife, arrived looking nice in black lace.

"Please come and sit in front. I've reserved you a place."

"No," she said shortly. "I'd prefer to sit at the back."

Within minutes her husband arrived carrying her shawl. "Is Maureen here?"

"Oh, please go away!" I said. "It's ladies only and they've all uncovered. I'll be in real trouble if you don't go."

"I'm loving it," he said, standing in the middle of the audience and turning slowly to gaze at a lot of deep *décolleté*.

"Give me the shawl," I demanded, snatching it from him. "And please go." I gave him a shove.

In the beam of light I thanked the audience for coming and everyone who had helped. I could hear voices in the surrounding bushes and realised that the Embassy men could not resist the spectacle, either.

"Next Tuesday, there will be a make-up demonstration in my house at 5pm as usual."

Maureen jumped up. "Oh no there won't," she announced. "These are my guests and everyone is coming to my house next time." And she sat down with a plonk.

Throughout the rest of our posting Oliver and I were invited into dozens of Saudi houses – once, unbelievably, we went to a family compound where the Saudi women and girls larked around in the swimming pool despite Oliver's presence. By the time we left the country, we had a list of 100 Saudi contacts to pass on to our successor.

UNDER THE SAUDI SUN

Jeddah is the commercial centre of Saudi Arabia but Riyadh, the capital, is where the political business happens, and we frequently visited the city, staying in the dismal Embassy villa.

Once we chose to take a taxi from Riyadh to Jeddah – about 1,000km. I was dreading this as I had heard so many stories about poorly maintained vehicles. I insisted before we started the journey that Oliver perform a charade of inspecting the vehicle to check that it was properly maintained. The driver ignored us. Winding his scarf round his head with only his eyes showing – as camel drivers do – he jumped into the old crate, and we thundered along the dead-straight tarmac strip laid across the desert. Visibility was nil because of the dust thrown up by approaching vehicles. Every so often we swerved violently onto the sand to avoid an oncoming lorry, and then back onto the strip.

"*Shway, shway,*" I shouted, wanting the driver to slow down. He kept turning round without decelerating, trying to understand what I was going on about. Finally, I just sat in the well of the vehicle and shut my eyes. Suddenly we came to a screeching halt. There, sinuously crossing the strip, were hundreds of camels, chewing in their supercilious manner and taking their time.

"Jolly lucky we didn't kill one," observed Oliver as we revved up for the final sprint home. "That would have cost us an arm and a leg."

One of our first trips out of Jeddah was over the inhospitable Hejaz mountains to Taif.

Dear Mum and Dad
We went to see an Arab family – refugees from Behan.
We sat on the floor sipping fizzy orange drinks and then went up to the women's quarters and the roof where Tom was made a great fuss of. He's had nightmares ever since. The women were like great black crows with their abiyahs blowing in the wind, so I don't blame him. Then we had a 'mutton grab' which was delicious – just us Europeans and the Arab men. Delicious hot chapatis and vegetables flavoured with cumin. Tom put his foot in the rice and I kept forgetting not to use my left hand but otherwise it went off all right. Afterwards we were sprayed with scent, which at least covered the lack of washing facilities …

Once during the Ambassador's absence when Oliver was *Chargé d'Affaires*, he was called to see the King who had moved up the mountains to his summer palace in Taif.

"You can all come," Oliver said magnanimously, "since Mohamed will drive us in the Austin Princess. But I'll sit in front to keep clean and you and Jaki will have to manage the boys in the back."

We packed a picnic with lots of bananas and water and set off. Halfway up the impressively engineered bin Laden Highway, Mohamed turned off the road, stopped, and opened the bonnet.

"Overheating. You have A/C or you have engine – which you like?"

So we continued climbing the vertiginous road with the windows open but little cool air. At the palace, Oliver jumped out, avoiding all sticky embraces.

"Take the women for their picnic," he instructed Mohamed, who immediately set off to the outskirts of town and deposited us on the municipal rubbish dump.

There was a little shade provided by a scattering of eucalyptus trees underneath which were piles of the usual domestic detritus, topped by thousands of goats' legs that still sported hair. (The animals must have been eaten at the post-Ramadan Eid celebration.) In discomfort, partly because there was nowhere to sit down and partly because of the swarms of flies, we ate our picnic quickly, then admitted to each other that we needed a pee. For a rubbish dump it was well populated with Arab men, so we summoned Mohamed and directed him to the hotel where we were to meet Oliver.

By then Jaki and I were smeared with sweat, grime and sticky bananas, which may explain the unhelpful reaction of the male receptionist. At least there was air conditioning in the tiny entrance hall, so we sat back trying to ignore our bladders. Mohamed thankfully was playing with the boys outside, probably allowing them to sit in the driving seat of the Austin Princess. A tall, handsome and perfumed Arab entered, swishing his robes behind him. I knew his face but could not recall who he was but on impulse I smiled and said,

"Hello, you may not remember me but ..."

"Mrs Miles. Of course. I have just enjoyed lunch with your charming husband."

The pleasantries continued until I burst out: "Help us please ..." The receptionist was told to accommodate us immediately. When I returned, Oliver was deep in conversation with the man who turned out to be Khalid Anani, the King's interpreter.

Jeddah is the nearest town to Mecca and Medina, the two holy cities, and when the Haj, or Pilgrimage, begins, Muslims from all over the world arrive. One year, out of the blue, a pilot phoned asking what he could bring me in his empty plane when he returned to collect his pilgrim passengers. I suggested a jar of horseradish sauce to make the meat more palatable.

A week later, he left a message to say that a crate of horseradish sauce awaited collection behind the reception desk of the downtown Red Sea Palace Hotel. Several weeks passed until I found somebody willing to fetch it by which time the crate had disappeared. The only thing that cheered me up was the thought of the thief's face as he dug deeply into a pot of horseradish sauce.

It was hazardous being a pilgrim because of the heat, crowds and emotional atmosphere around the holy Ka'ba in Mecca. Many pilgrims died of heatstroke. Oliver discussed this with my father, who was an Environmental Physiologist with a long-term interest and expertise in the effect of heat on the body. As a result in 1980, he and a Sudanese doctor named Mustafa Khogali devised a mobile unit which ensured rapid body cooling without vasoconstriction. We always laughed at my father's Heath Robinson devices but these units have saved many lives. They still remain the preferred means of treating heat stroke, and in Saudi Arabia are stored in purpose-built casualty stations along the Haj route.

Saudi Arabia seemed to have an especially virulent effect on personal relationships. One Embassy couple permanently swapped partners with a couple in the British community. Another wife became pregnant by someone else's husband and lay for hours in the broiling sun trying to abort the foetus, or to punish herself. There were signs of stress and depression amongst the secretarial staff, too.

Then the Ambassador and his wife went peculiar. Oliver had already repatriated one depressed Head of Mission. This couple were probably also depressed but complained of physical symptoms. The Ambassador was shipped back to St Thomas' Hospital in London for what turned out to be a false alarm. Maureen took to her bed with back pain and demanded that the wives set up a rota of care in place of the FCO-appointed nurse. I used my pregnancy as an excuse but several wives complied even to the extent of spending the night on call in the Residence. One requirement was to 'hang her on the back of the door' strapped into some contraption designed to stretch her spine. She was not a small woman and this must have been an ordeal.

It was not a happy Embassy.

Many of the Embassy wives found paid work, which left a couple of us on the empty compound looking after their children. I was desperate for a job and managed a little invigilation for the British Council. One day just as the lift to their offices reached the third floor there was a power cut preventing the doors from opening more than a few inches. I managed to squeeze through the gap otherwise I suppose I might have suffered a horrible death as the electricity was not restored in that part of town for 48 hours.

For a short time I held a teaching post in the Women's University, but perhaps because my essay titles were probably subversive I was told I could remain only if I surrendered my diplomatic immunity – an unthinkable option in the authoritarian and unpredictable Saudi environment. Sadly I resigned the post, although this was tempered with relief because the journey to and from the Women's University caused me such anxiety: I was never sure if I would arrive on time or how I would get home.

I did however manage to persuade the Consul to allow me to visit Jeddah prison, but this only happened once:

Dear Mum and Dad
I've just been to see my poor old prisoner. There's only one British person in Jeddah jail and he was conned into bringing in drugs. He's been inside for a year. When he is sentenced, it will be for 15 years, I think. He's quite remarkable in many ways, not least his cheerful and constructive attitude. He's started to teach his prison governor English. It's odd to go into an all-male institution here, but nobody bats an eyelid.

We've been invited to the execution of a butcher who went berserk in the suq and killed an English businessman. Of course we are not going ... although it is for our benefit – Arab justice decrees that we should witness the punishment.

*The head of police was most insistent that representatives
from the British Embassy should be there ...*

Just at this time, Oliver had slipped a disc and had taken to
lying on the floor. He was adamant, however, that we should
honour our invitation for a drink to two visiting British MPs.
They were a bit nonplussed to hear Oliver's voice coming
from behind the sofa, but it soon became clear that they were
already in shock. Gabbling simultaneously, they fell on the
whisky bottle.

"You'll never guess ..."

"They took us to an execution."

"And since we were guests of honour we were pushed to
the front."

"They wouldn't take no for an answer. It all happened so
quickly we ... ugh."

"We were covered in blood. God it was sickening."

Our Eritrean maid was the shop steward on the compound, so
there was no question of dismissing her. Her face was set in
a habitual expression of haughty contempt. Once I found her
teaching the boys how to put plastic bags over their heads. She
was a strange woman.

Some people hired local cooks and Oliver was keen that we
should try one.

"He says he's cooked for the British Army in the
Hindu Kush."

On cue a tiny, skinny and wizened old man with no teeth and
an unmistakable tremble hobbled out of our kitchen wearing a
filthy nylon thobe. "Good evening, Madam. I am Ali and I am
here tomorrow for trial period."

"Right, Ali. What do you like to cook?"

"My speciality is ..." – he paused for dramatic effect – "...

spun sugar baskets. I put fresh fruit inside. Once I put in a live bird and all the dinner guests clapped."

"Ali, I really just need you to cook for the family."

"All right, I understand. What do you want? Steak and kidney pie?"

"If you can find any steak or kidney or flour for the pastry, I should be delighted."

"No problem. What time you like lunch?"

The next morning we were woken by a massive explosion. Oliver ran downstairs to discover Ali, not badly burned, but concerned for his dignity as his nylon *thobe* had shrivelled up to nothing. He had left the gas taps on all night and when he struck a match, a ball of fire engulfed him. That he was more of a liability than an asset was accepted and Ali left. So I never had the experience of eating steak and kidney pie in Jeddah.

Food was always a problem and finding ingredients demanded ingenuity.

Dear Mum and Dad
Please could you send us packets of herb seeds, rosemary, basil and oregano ... Everything tends to taste stale and needs a lot of flavouring. Luckily, the onions here are strong. A cook brought us some white flour for bread but it was so alive with worms and weevils, which have their own distinctive taste – I chucked it. The brown flour seems better so I have had several baking sessions. I've also been making yoghurt as someone gave me some Bulgarian culture ...

There was also the everlasting problem of physically reaching a shop. Once a week half a dozen wives and assorted kids would pile into an old Land Cruiser. It was driven by Saif whom we wives christened 'Unsafe' because of his hit-or-miss driving style. He used a sock to pull out the choke and another to block the petrol tank. Sadly, he was declared blind soon after I left Jeddah.

The vegetable market sold high quality produce. I always bought from the same stallholder where we had a running joke in elementary Arabic and English about my uncanny capacity to estimate weights accurately. Unfortunately he interpreted this as an invitation to a closer relationship and began running his hands over me. I responded when he climbed a ladder by putting my hand up his *thobe* and scrabbling around. It gave him the fright of his life.

People going on leave were always asked to bring goods back. I gathered a large order for Marmite and gelatine from the British community. Once in England I went into Sainsbury's and piled quantities of each item into my trolley. The woman on the check-out stared at my shopping for some time and then finally said, "Do tell me the recipe".

The Saudis knew we imported alcohol and once, referring to a consignment at the docks, informed us "your typewriters are leaking". But our Embassy was careful not to attract any opprobrium, unlike another European mission which was caught selling quantities of the stuff.

Many Saudis hoped to be beneficiaries of Embassy hospitality. So did the British community, some of whom manufactured their own liquor. Rumours circulated about parts of stills being confiscated at airports, and of people going blind through consumption of methyl alcohol. No doubt angling for an invitation to an Embassy function, a long-resident expatriate couple invited us to dinner.

"Welcome," shouted the host as he threw open the door, and then whispered, "be assured that there is more to this humble abode than meets the eye." The assembled expat company was sipping genteelly from crystal glasses. "Now, what can I offer you? Whisky, gin …?"

"Good heavens," I exclaimed, "how on earth …?"

"Ask no questions and I'll tell you no lies. Let's just say the answer lies not a million miles away." He nodded in the direction of a bedroom and handed us printed menus decorated with trailing vines advising us that the casseroled chicken would be enlivened with Chateau Margaux 1976.

At the end of the meal, he commanded our full attention: "I'd like to introduce our newest acquisition: apricot brandy." With a flourish he produced two matching bottles sporting identical labels and poured colourless liquid into Waterford tumblers. It was delicious, tasted unmistakably of apricots and felt as if an electric cattle prod had seared my brain.

"Do tell me how you find the bottles and such authentic labels?"

"That's mine to know and you to wonder."

We wandered home and tumbled into bed. In the middle of the night I woke up suddenly, staring into blackness.

"Oliver, I've gone blind."

"Rubbish. There's no moon tonight."

Being a BBC radio *aficionado* in England, I found the silence in our Jeddah house oppressive. At first we had no radio because it was stuck in Customs for months. When it finally arrived I found the reception was so poor that it was redundant.

Saudi TV broadcast Muslim prayers all day. Oliver occasionally caught an Arabic news bulletin but there was no schedule. The Americans managed to sell the Saudis a soap opera on the condition that no scene showed a man and woman together, or any drinking; occasionally the censor would slip up and the screen would be plunged into blackness. But dubbed and censored soaps held no interest for me.

The censors' handiwork was everywhere. A one-piece swimsuit was often meticulously hand drawn in black ink over a newspaper photograph of a bikini-clad model. It must have been terribly labour intensive to expurgate every imported publication. A friend who worked for an advertising agency got into trouble with her printed advertisement that said "New Fashion Revolution!" because the word 'revolution' is not permitted in the Kingdom. Our newspapers resembled doilies because so much had been excised. The Military Attaché wrote to the editor of *The Times* asking him to stop printing advertisements for holidays to Israel on the back of the crossword puzzle because it was impossible to solve when half the clues were missing.

A local English-language newspaper, the *Arab News*, pre-empted the censor by printing a photograph of the British racing driver James Hunt triumphantly knocking back a magnum of champagne, with the caption: "James Hunt celebrates with a bottle of milk."

I too had a brush with the censor. Our entertainment was necessarily of the home-spun variety, and an Embassy carol-singing party was proposed. This, to the Saudis, was proselytising and strictly forbidden, as was Christmas. Nevertheless, on Christmas Eve a strange little group wearing woolly hats, gloves and Wellington boots in a temperature of 100 degrees assembled in my house. Frances Moore, wife of a senior diplomat, announced the itinerary:

"First we go to the German Ambassador, then the American Military Attaché, then the Canadian Ambassador and lastly next door."

"Not our Military Attaché!" I exclaimed. (I was quite terrified of Brian in those days.) The German Ambassador also looked formidable, being a tall grey-haired Prussian type but he was very welcoming, probably because his wife had left him for the holidays.

"I have zis magnificent blue spruce tree."

We stared at the real Christmas tree touching the ceiling of his elegant drawing room, smelling of resin, and with a fat white candle attached to each branch. My parents had sent us a tiny artificial tree as I had not been able to find a plastic tree and decorations in Basingstoke in July.

"You all have doughnuts and Sekt, ze German champagne? Gut. Now ve shut ze lights and everybody lights his candle."

"Are you sure? It might catch fire."

"Don't be such a bore."

For a few seconds we were transported a million miles from the real Jeddah with its thumping traffic outside. And then the tree caught fire. Frances cleverly set up a line of people and in orderly fashion we passed buckets up and down.

The Ambassador doused the tree until – forlorn and blackened – it stood in a huge puddle. He sadly mopped the floor.

"You zing a little carol now to make me feel better – yes?"

The American Military Attaché was all smiling bonhomie as his wife rushed about the lavishly decorated house handing out egg nog and Southern date cake. As we left, a posse of gum-chewing, bobby-socked teenagers who had been hanging over the banisters attached themselves to us in a line of cars. The Canadian Embassy was in darkness. We were just about to leave when someone said, "Is that Chopin?"

"I had forgotten that he was a highbrow."

Then the light snapped on. "Gluwein and mince pies anyone?" cried Mrs Shenstone hospitably. "Let's hear you!"

After a decent effort to sing while feeling rather nauseous, the motorcade snaked off towards our Military Attaché's house. "Frances, you go first to explain," I insisted.

Brian slid back the French window to reveal a classy cocktail party in full swing. "Good God. Just look at you," he exclaimed, appalled.

A strange sight of munchkins insouciantly blowing gum bubbles and adults sweating under bobble hats met the eyes of his polished, tuxedo-wearing guests.

"All right, just one, and then it's out with the lot of you."

Around that time I was writing intermittently under the name of 'Ursula Prune' for the *Saudi Gazette*, an English-language newspaper, and couldn't resist getting an account of this illegal escapade in print. I knew the censor would not approach me directly; instead, he phoned Oliver and with difficulty read out "Sekt, er, egg nog, gluwein … what is this?"

"Don't worry old chap, all harmless," said my loyal spouse.

It was published uncensored.

In London, I had been assured by the Foreign Office medical adviser that malaria did not exist in Saudi Arabia but two members of the Embassy, who were inveterate campers, caught it. I pressed Oliver to ask London to send out some prophylactic Paludrine. None came. Some weeks later, I happened to notice a bottle, admittedly small but nevertheless Paludrine, on the Ambassador's dining table. It turned out that London had been supplying him and his wife but not the rest of us. I was incandescent. Eventually the FCO relented, complaining sulkily about the cost.

There were constant shortages and frustrations of every sort:

Dear Mum and Dad
We've had a rough time recently. No water on the compound – had to drink the swimming pool. Now water's being brought in by bowser, dark brown and in limited quantity. I stockpiled a quantity of flour as no bread is being made … Everybody is waiting for something …

Dear Mum and Dad
No water again today as I discovered when I was trying to wash up a post-concert party – curry dishes – at 2am. When a bowser finally did arrive there was no oil to heat it – in Saudi Arabia! – so we all washed in cold … the air-conditioning went off as this is linked to the water-cooling system. We've been in a fine state …

Dear Mum and Dad
The funniest story I've heard for ages came from a nice Embassy couple who live off the compound. Their predecessor ordered a telephone two years ago … Last week, great rejoicing, the phone was installed, but the only place it would work was on the roof. Maggie said it was jolly hard to hear it ringing and quite uncomfortable for Ken when called out at night as he doesn't wear anything in bed. I have visions of Ken naked under a starry sky sending telegrams to Whitehall – they'd never believe it …

Dear Mum and Dad
ICI are apparently hoping for a contract to kill rats, flies,
cats, dogs etc. But unfortunately not in Jeddah ...

Many wives were worried about the wild dogs and cats which strolled unhindered around the compound. One wife, Mary Lewty, was so anxious that her pet cat did not catch some dread disease from these alley cats that she asked her husband to invite the Americans, who, she presumed, had guns, to come and shoot them. The Americans refused on the grounds that they could carry guns on their own compound where they exterminated the wild dogs and cats, but not on the street between their Embassy and ours. So the problem remained until one day I met Mary looking hot but happy.

"I was going to wash my dining room net curtains but then I had a better idea. I went round the compound catching all the strays with them, and I've put them in a diplomatic bag by the dustbins."

"Where they will be released and the problem will start all over again." Which is exactly what happened.

Woodrow Wyatt, a Labour politician, visited Jeddah at this time. Impressed by the Embassy work being done in difficult circumstances he took it upon himself to make some suggestions to the FCO for improving the post: e.g. 10 Range Rovers and a Life Peer as Ambassador. The reply from London was so misleading that Oliver drafted a telegram saying he would have liked to have circulated WW's congratulations to the staff but felt the Foreign Secretary's reply would have damaged morale.

Eventually I got so fed up with my restricted lifestyle that I decided to phone my father and ask him to send money for the fare back to England. I forgot that, this being Saudi Arabia, there was bound to be an insurmountable obstacle. The Embassy telephone operator informed me that he had to have my husband's written permission before he could put through a long-distance call. I confessed my plan to Oliver who persuaded me that it was quite out of the question so against my better judgment, I stayed.

At the time I was pregnant and desperately needed the baby things that I had sent from England but which the Saudi Customs officials had impounded. Self-help was the only answer. I had friends in a firm of posh American lawyers who were perpetually flying back and forth to London. They refused to transport a pram for me but they did help another Embassy wife, Jean Brown. She worked as a doctor and urgently needed someone to take an eye to St Thomas' Hospital for an autopsy. I appealed to my American lawyer friend, Bill Morrison, who agreed to help. He has chided me ever since because the formaldehyde leaked and left a stain on his new leather briefcase.

Just occasionally something unexpected happened to lift my flagging spirits. After a unique invitation to a Saudi dinner party, the hostess, Leila Ali Reza, phoned. She had overheard me admiring the roses that festooned her house.

"I am so pleased you enjoyed the garden," she cooed. "I simply adore roses and order bushes from Holland every year. Would you like me to get you some?" This was quite unprecedented. Few people rang me at home, and never Saudis. I suspected she ordered bushes by the hundred and was probably also fairly profligate with water. "How many would you like?"

"Er ... three?"

"You mean three dozen?"

"No, let me start with three bushes and see if I can make them grow."

True to her word, three rose bushes arrived. So I was then faced with the problem of gardening without water. The Ambassador had just sent round an order forbidding baths. (We noticed, however, his lawn spray constantly played in his lush green garden). I was not sure what would happen if our neighbour, the Military Attaché, caught me. He had already made a tiny reference to the children running around outside his bedroom early in the morning. In an uncharacteristic act of protest against our way of life, Tom, aged three, had dug a large hole, regrettably close to the Colonel's French windows, and buried our expensively engraved blank personal invitation cards and envelopes. After some active sleuthing, I surreptitiously dug them up again.

In short, I felt slightly paranoid about our neighbours. So in the early hours I crept out and planted the roses, quietly tipping a bucket of dirty washing up water over them. To my horror a tell-tale tide mark still remained in the morning. I waited to see what would happen. One plant eventually produced a bright pink bloom.

The Colonel hove into view. "That's an impressive flower," he commented as he strode home for lunch.

Another unexpected bonus occurred on the same day that termites chewed through several compound front doors. In going to inspect mine, I stamped on a large brown scorpion basking on the front door mat. Oliver and I then went for a walk along the seashore. When we got back my sister-in-law, Linda, was standing outside. I thought the sun had affected me. I never saw Linda in England, so why would I here?

"I was hoping you'd be back as John's at the airport." Oliver's brother, John, was a commercial pilot.

"Has something awful happened?"

"We had to make an unscheduled landing and it looks as if we'll be stuck for a couple of days."

Having delivered bathroom fittings to East Africa, John had loaded up several tons of pineapples destined for Marks & Spencer, a forbidden company in Saudi Arabia.

"The air conditioning on the plane has given up so you can imagine the smell," said John when he arrived. "The sooner we can get out of here the better. We thought we'd land in Jeddah because the fuel is cheap – oh, and of course to see you."

Oliver canvassed some of our Saudi friends who were in retail or import but no one would touch the cargo.

"I am allowed to take two individual fruit off the plane," John said.

"Good. We're giving a buffet supper tomorrow so let's serve them. I don't think Saudis have ever seen pineapples before."

We used the pineapples as a spectacular centrepiece where they were gratifyingly remarked upon. The Saudi guests poked them suspiciously and then bravely agreed to sample the strange-looking fruit. The following year Jeddah shops were full of pineapples. So I stake a claim to having first introduced the pineapple into Saudi Arabia.

On Friday May 20 1977 we were invited to spend the day with the Husseini family in their house at the Creek. Passing the old, closed-up Jeddah airport we were surprised to see an Olympic airliner. We wondered how it had landed without a control tower and lights, and how it would ever take off again.

"Trust the Greeks" we sniggered, having had some intimation of our next posting. During that afternoon we noticed helicopters repeatedly circling low over the sea but we could not discover what was going on.

Soon, rumours started sweeping the Embassy about Friday's events. It emerged that 19-year-old Princess Misha'al – great niece of King Abdul Aziz, the founder of modern Saudi Arabia – had faked a drowning so that she could escape from Saudi Arabia with the lover she had met at school in Lebanon. The couple was caught trying to leave the country and tried for adultery although neither was married. The Princess was shot and he, having witnessed her execution, was beheaded with a sword. But this was all kept secret. A film, *Death of a Princess*, was later released to American and British TV networks which led the outraged Saudis to expel the British Ambassador.

In time, we received confirmation of our next posting – Athens. Officially we had earned two months' home leave, but we had been in a 'push-me-pull-you' situation between two Ambassadors who were prioritising their own needs at our expense. Since we were forced to remain in Jeddah six weeks longer than planned, we lost all but a fortnight's break.

Our Hampshire house had been re-let and we were homeless. Again I threw myself on the kindness of our American friend, Bill Morrison, who in an unguarded moment, had confided that he owned a flat in Chelsea that we might use. The flat was in the basement of a smart block, but the enormous belching boiler which served all the apartments was situated at the core of our flat, with our rooms encircling it. I became worried about the possibility of carbon monoxide poisoning and the thought that if we needed to get out in an emergency, the boys would be trapped behind the boiler. Regarding the place as a potential death trap, I instructed everyone to keep their windows open.

On the second day in Chelsea we visited the dentist. He became concerned when Tom, aged four, reported a stiff neck. Knowing we had just returned from Saudi Arabia he urged us to get him checked out for meningitis. I protested that the stiff neck had been caused by a draught from an open window, but nevertheless, Tom was admitted to the Westminster Children's Hospital. They insisted on performing a lumbar puncture which meant he had to stay in hospital for three days. I was given a bed there, too. It was a worrying time. I shared a room with a woman whose child was far sicker than mine, but I could not sleep and was up at 5am wandering through the empty London streets. To our relief Tom was discharged, battered and shaken but thankfully well.

GREECE: GLADRAGS
AND COCKTAILS

When we emerged from the escalator at Athens airport I brought up the rear, looking drab and exhausted. It was not surprising that suave, silver-haired Tim Everard, the Commercial Counsellor, effusively welcomed Jaki, our mother's help, mistakenly thinking that she was the new Counsellor's wife. He drove us to our upmarket apartment in Athens overlooking the Royal Gardens where we lived for the first three months. The maid insisted on unpacking our luggage.

"When will Madam's clothes be arriving?" she enquired.

"These are my clothes," I replied.

During our two-week home leave, I had intended to spruce myself up and buy some new clothes; in Jeddah, I had lopped off my hair myself so that it had no shape or style. But all that went by the board as we took a week's farm holiday so that Tom could regain his strength. Athens was an elegant posting but it was difficult to find reasonably priced smart clothes there. Many Greek women had 'little dressmakers' but they also spent time and money shopping in London or Paris. Having used our truncated leave either in hospital or on a farm I had missed my hoped-for opportunity to smarten up, and for a year had to make do, often wearing the kaftan I had bought for Jeddah nightlife from John Lewis' dressing-gown department three years earlier.

Oliver's job carried the unwieldy title of 'Political Counsellor and Consul General'. Greece, a conservative and formal society, in 1977 was dominated by a gerontocracy. I was 32 years old but our social life was invariably spent with people well over 70. Naturally I made friends with other mothers at the school gates but they were not regarded as 'useful contacts', so we did not entertain them, nor did they invite us to their homes. After a year of unadulterated exposure to Grannies and Grandpas I implored Oliver to give a 'young people's party'. He concocted a list of fifty year olds whom we invited to a buffet supper. Over drinks I noticed a rather self-important industrialist craning his neck to assess whether the guest list sufficiently reflected his status, then he excused himself before dinner saying that he was obliged to attend an old boys' reunion.

Greeks are immensely hospitable, which means a lot of reciprocating. This is exceedingly difficult without a dedicated staff, which only the Ambassador had. I struggled to meet the demands while caring for three small boys and (from November 1979) a baby girl. I was exhausted most of the time and the last thing I felt like doing was to cater for grand parties, but I had no choice. I was always terrified something would go wrong, although by dint of rigorous planning, it usually didn't.

In 1965, King Constantine had dismissed George Papandreou as Prime Minister and appointed a more right-wing government which lasted shakily for 18 months. In 1967, elections were called with the expectation of a left-wing victory under Papandreou, but the right-wing Junta pre-empted that with a *coup d'etat*, and the King fled into exile.

The Junta's own downfall seven years later occurred because they tried to take advantage of the strong Greek Cypriot movement towards 'Enosis', or union with Greece. The preferred candidate for their puppet president was probably our Greek Cypriot friend Michael Triantafillides, who happened to be away from the island at the time and would very likely have refused the offer. Nikos Sampson, the terrorist (from whom I had shielded my dance partner), was installed, which did not add to the gravitas or respectability of the coup. Turkey, alarmed at this development, invaded Cyprus. The Junta collapsed in 1974. Sampson disappeared and Makarios was restored as President of Cyprus. Karamanlis returned from exile in Paris to be elected Prime Minister of Greece.

When we arrived in Athens in 1977, we found a nation in shock, attempting to repair damage to its psyche and restore financial confidence. After more than a century of trying to establish a monarchy Greece had reverted to democratic republicanism. There was still a strong Communist threat but the middle ground held sway with a democratic two-party system.

The infrastructure was not strong and many people in the private sector avoided paying taxes. There was over-employment in business and the civil service. Roads needed repair and there were daily strikes. The first time Oliver tried to commute to the Embassy from the suburbs he found that no buses were running. He was just considering how to get to work when an army lorry drove up and he was hauled aboard the flat-bed truck by friendly Greeks.

While we lived in central Athens I used to take Hugh to play in the Royal Gardens. Another mum was doing the same and we became friends. She and her husband lived in a neighbouring apartment and had a son aged nine months, the same age as Hugh. Ann Atlamazoglou was an American heiress who had first visited Athens as a teenager. She reminded me of a Henry James character. She had espied Stelios, a handsome but impoverished Greek, in a lift, vowed she would marry him, and did. She put him through the first two years of architectural school before he quit.

After a few years of marriage he fulfilled a dream by designing their magnificent villa high up on the rocks on the island of Spetses. They often invited us to stay. The only problem was that Stelios had miscalculated the space required for the doors to open fully so that we had to make a detour through the garden when carrying a baby or a tray.

A sheaf of invitations was waiting when we arrived in Athens. The first was from the Dutch Ambassador, who lived just round the corner. That evening Oliver was reclining virtually naked on the bed and Jaki was in the next room, fiddling with the invitation cards.

"What do you suppose '*cravat noir*' means?" she mused out loud.

Oliver sat up, galvanised. "My God, is that tonight? I haven't got it." Our heavy baggage had mysteriously gone to Beirut.

"It's OK," I said. "I was speaking to Peter Williams today, and he said if we needed anything, I should phone. He's about your size." Peter was the Naval Attaché.

"He's probably going to the same party."

I rang him. He was going to a party, but not ours, and was happy to lend his dinner jacket. He asked me to meet him outside the Alpha Beta Supermarket – about three miles away through heavy traffic – in 20 minutes. There was no option. The Dutch Ambassador's party started in half an hour. I seized the keys to our new car, which I had never driven, and sped off into the wild Greek traffic. From previous visits I had a vague notion of Athens' geography, and made my way up the huge highway, trying to work the lights, indicators and windscreen wipers while playing dodgems with the other cars. The supermarket eventually loomed into view and there was Peter, impatiently holding out the suit.

It was quite difficult to do a U-turn but time was short. Then I noticed the petrol gauge pointing at zero. When the British Embassy building came into view I thought it better to abandon the car in case it ran out of fuel on the four-lane highway. I had the mistaken impression that our flat was just a moment's walk away from the Office. Holding the dinner suit as carefully as possible, I ran across the busy main road and dived down some side streets. Puffing and panting I chanced to pass by the Dutch Ambassador's Residence just as some elegant people alighted serenely from their limousines. As I cantered past in my jeans and T-shirt, I thoughtlessly waved and called, "Back in a minute".

Oliver was still reclining on the bed. I tossed the hanger at him and with infuriating slowness he started to dress while I dashed around with garments and lipstick. There was a palpable frisson as we were the last to arrive at the Dutch Embassy. I think some of the guests may have recognised me.

The British Ambassador, Sir Brooks Richards, was grand but affable with a distinguished war record in Special Operations Executive (SOE). I found his wife inscrutable but tough. In late middle age, she had ridden a mule through the mountains in Northern Greece to visit villages cut off by the winter snow. In those days the few roads in Northern Greece were pretty inaccessible by car, even at less hostile times of year.

The Residence was an imposing house which had been built by the eminent Greek Prime Minister, Eleftherios Venizelos, in the 1930s. It was said to have 100 rooms. When the Greek Government refused to give him a State funeral his wife, who had intended to bequeath the house to the Greek Nation for the use of future Prime Ministers, sold it to the British Government at a knock-down price. The drawing room walls were lined with shelves which the Ambassador had filled with a collection of ancient Chinese porcelain. I think he may have been rather taken aback when, while I was admiring this, I commented that were I ever to be in his position I would have a bit of a problem as my ornaments consisted of the alabaster head Oliver had brought back from Aden and a three legged silver duck which we had recently bought in an Egyptian suq. Luckily by the time we moved into the house some years later, it had been extensively refurbished and the shelves had gone.

The first time we were invited to the British Ambassador's Residence there was a mammoth thunderstorm and Athens was plunged into darkness.

Dear Mum and Dad

We had no electricity between 8pm and 10am … It was the night of the Ambassador's posh party and I'd intended to dress up but we had to get ready by striking matches … so we snatched whatever we could find. The first thing O did when he arrived at the Residence, which must have its own generator as it was all lit up, was to check whether he was wearing brown or black shoes with his DJ. It took us an hour to drive there – five minutes' walk normally. The traffic was chaotic, the roads badly flooded and the rain didn't let up. We ended up driving on the pavement like everyone else. We arrived second to last but Paddy Leigh Fermor (the writer) didn't arrive at all …

At another British Embassy function, the butler hung all the coats on a rail inside the ballroom. At the end of the party, seeing me crossing the floor he called out loudly: "The nylon, Madam?" and brought out my *faux* fur from where it nestled amongst the minks and the foxes. The next day, contrite and sober, he presented me with a bunch of wilted lettuce seedlings.

Our apartment in central Athens was bang next to the Greek President's house. He was fussy about his afternoon siesta, but our little boys came home from school wanting to lark about. These two circumstances were incompatible and so I sought permission to move. After a short search I found an elegant old villa outside Athens in the suburb of Kifissia, which the Embassy agreed to rent for us.

We were advised that it would be prudent to remove the American Military Attaché's brass plate on the gatepost, as the Americans were not popular. (There was a widespread but unsubstantiated belief that the right-wing rule of the Junta had been supported by the United States.) We had barely got 'British Political Counsellor and Consul General' nailed up when we had to take it down again because Irish terrorists had recently murdered the British Ambassador in The Hague and were rumoured to be spreading through Europe.

Our house was an imposing one with a history; Prime Minister Karamanlis had spent his honeymoon there when Kifissia was still a village. Kifissia stands in an elevated position at the western end of the Penteli mountains which makes it a cool summer resort but bitterly cold in winter. People are often surprised at the harsh Mediterranean winters, probably because they mostly visit Greece in the summer.

Dear Mum and Dad
The weather is freezing again – we had snow and a huge thunderstorm that was so noisy we did not hear the sound of pine trees being torn up by the roots and smashing across the garden. The terrace was standing vertical when we looked out at breakfast time, and all the tiles will have to be relaid …

Across the road was a dry cleaner. One day I was queuing to collect my clothes. As I shifted from foot to foot I glanced over my shoulder and practically died, as there behind me in the queue was a five and a half foot dancing bear, his muzzle about six inches from my ear. I glanced nervously at the other customers but their expressions were uniformly impassive.

As soon as we moved in, a charismatic member of the Embassy and long-term resident of Athens, Eddie Duckworth, persuaded Oliver to adopt a dog from the sanctuary. Judy was totally unsuitable – a pure white, pedigree Samoyed with a very bad temper. On one occasion I was horrified to find a lady guest who was waiting in the drawing room pinned to the floor by the triumphant animal. Doubtless Judy had been discarded by a Greek family who had been seduced by her glamour, but she needed constant grooming, and Oliver soon found the chore better left to me.

Dozens of tortoises wandered around the garden. Judy would spend the morning spitefully turning them onto their backs and I would spend the afternoon righting them. I wondered how I might ever be released from this tiresome duty. Then one day she gave birth to three puppies and went mad. First she ate them and then became so aggressive that we knew we could not keep her with small children around, and Eddie reluctantly agreed to return her to the dogs' home, not a moment too soon for me.

The villa's garden was lush and romantic. There were apricot, pomegranate and lemon trees and, in spring, a carpet of wild flowers. I imagined women with bustles and parasols strolling around or watching tennis from the stone terrace under the mulberry trees. A rubbish pit had replaced the tennis court, but the garden remained an oasis of calm away from the unremitting roar of Athens' traffic.

"What's in that grey bungalow?" I asked our landlord one day, indicating a dreary-looking concrete building amongst the anemones, with formidably barred windows.

"Come. I'll show you my museum."

He unlocked the heavy door to reveal an Aladdin's cave. Carpets, icons and pictures in glorious jewel colours shone through the gloom. He dazzled us with this treasure, which consisted of ancient illuminated Bibles and Korans, and the first printed edition of Homer.

Once, when his wife was away, the Ambassador, Oliver and I attended a lunch given by a closet homosexual for the departing Brazilian Ambassador and his wife. The party for about a dozen people took place in a surprisingly dilapidated house. As usual I was by far the youngest. I remarked on the impressive number of books to a small Greek woman dressed in black with huge horn-rimmed spectacles.

"We have so many books at home we even have them in our lavatory," she boasted.

"Is your husband a book seller?" I asked in an attempt to get the conversation going.

She eyed me coldly. "No, he was the last Prime Minister."

Seated at table, a large white ball was presented for the first course. The Brazilian Ambassador's wife masterfully dug in and we discovered it was a delicious local cheese with a texture like mushrooms, called *anthotiro*. Then a second white ball arrived.

The Brazilian wife said, "That was delicious; but no more thank you."

The host replied, "But this is the main course. It is quite different."

It turned out to be chicken and rice moulded to the size of a football. After we had eaten that, another white football arrived. It was vanilla ice cream. Back in the Ambassador's Rolls we speculated on the possible meaning of the three white balls.

"Might it have some reference to our host's sexuality?" mused the Ambassador.

"Or the Beautiful Game?" observed Oliver.

We also dined with the Chinese Ambassador. On arrival, we were encouraged to admire a two-sided embroidery of a cat where 120 shades of white silk thread made the fur look very realistic. I sat next to the Ambassador who insisted on serving me from the large segmented dish in the middle of the table. The only recognisable food was the delicious-looking prawns, but he piled my plate with some stuff resembling translucent rubber bands with the consistency of hair. When invited to a second helping I indicated that the prawns would be very acceptable now that I had politely eaten my way through the strange dish.

"So you liked the jellyfish?" enquired the Ambassador conversationally.

The Cypriot Ambassador, who was sitting next to me, gasped: "Jellyfish!" He clapped his hand over his mouth and dashed from the room.

The Embassy and its staff fielded a constant flow of MPs and other official visitors. David Mellor, MP for Putney, came accompanied by his political agent, who happened to be my godparents' son, and his wife. Our car had sprung a leak so the Consul volunteered to drive us to a *taverna* for dinner.

As we prepared to get into his estate car we realised our seating predicament. Julian and Frieda were aged, Oliver had injured his back, I was eight months pregnant and the Consul was the only person insured to drive the car. To his credit, David Mellor cheerfully folded himself into the boot of the vehicle while the rest of us sat in comfort in the seats.

Another time, the International Monetary Fund held a dinner in Athens for Finance Ministers, one of whom was Denis Healey, the Chancellor of the Exchequer. As we were leaving he reeled up to us and said, "I have a joke to tell you. I was sitting next to this Japanese banker and I was a bit shocked when he said the Common Market was a 'flea market'. I was just composing my riposte when he added: 'A velly flea market.' That's a good 'un isn't it? Hahaha."

Although we loved our Kifissia house, it was not very big and its layout was inflexible when it came to entertaining. There was no guest accommodation and certainly no *en suite* bedroom apart from our own and the maid's room. Having grandees to stay without notice was a nightmare, as I wrote home:

Dear Mum and Dad
Out of the blue the Duke of Norfolk came to stay on his
way back from the Pope's funeral … I put him in Athina's
room as it has a bathroom attached. It appealed to my
warped sense of humour to have the Duke stay in the
maid's room. It also kept him away from Hugh, who's
been having the Terrible Twos which involves midnight
roamings and lots of tantrums …

On another occasion, Yehudi Menuhin arrived in Athens on a Saturday when all the domestic staff were off duty, bringing with him two elderly cousins of the Queen. The Ambassador and his wife cobbled together some lunch and the rest of us were instructed to turn up afterwards at the enormous Herodou Atticou amphitheatre, for an impromptu concert where we sat, an insignificant little bunch, on the edge of the front row.

Menuhin performed accompanied by barking dogs, police sirens and ceaseless traffic noise, while a group of chattering tourists traipsed over the monument quite unaware of the grandeur of the occasion. A few weeks later another sudden 'Royal Command' brought us scuttling to the Grande Bretagne Hotel to meet Margot Fonteyn, who was in Athens to accept an honour from the Greek government. Nobody had forewarned the British Embassy. She did not offer to dance.

St Catherine's British Embassy School was founded in 1956 in the Residence garden by Lady (Catherine) Peake, the wife of the-then British Ambassador. Oliver, as chairman of governors, had to deliver a speech at the opening of a new building in front of the whole school and a group of dignitaries, including Mrs Averoff, the imposing wife of the Greek Minister of Defence. I persuaded Oliver that since the majority of his audience would be under 11, he should compose a humorous poem for the occasion. It took a whole weekend to write and he was pretty nervous when it came to delivery in case the audience felt it was insufficiently serious. But he received a positive reception and Mrs Averoff drew him to one side to tell him that her husband Evangelos was sorry to have missed it.

She explained that they had just been with the rest of the Greek Cabinet to scatter Maria Callas' ashes at sea. Television crews were filming and at the last minute the crew insisted that the boat be turned round because the light was wrong. The Captain's objections were overruled and the ashes were emptied over the side. The wind blew the ashes straight back over the mourners. "Poor Evangeli has been coughing all night," said Mrs Averoff.

BUCKINGHAM PALACE, A
BABY AND KISSING HANDS
WITH THE QUEEN

As we were leaving Athens for our mid-tour leave we were told that we had been invited to a garden party at Buckingham Palace. This would take place a few days after our return. Along with all the other things to be fitted into a short space of time I had to find something suitable to wear. I was six months pregnant.

The nearest shops to our remote Hampshire house included, bizarrely, a draper's. As we drove past I noticed in their window a flowing pastel Indian cotton dress, perfect for a heavily pregnant woman on a summer's day. I ran in and bought it while the rest of the family sat complaining in the car. I chopped off the bottom of the long skirt and used it to swathe my straw sunhat in a bandeau that matched my dress. Thus attired, I set off to visit the Queen.

The day of the Royal Garden Party was hot. A genteel clattering of hundreds of teacups and a buzz of conversation mingled with the band's rendition of *Iolanthe*. The Royal Standard fluttered from the roof, and a queue of politely chattering, florally dressed women snaked endlessly from the Ladies loo at the end of the lake. There was only one solution to my urgent need and that was to poke my head through the flap of the marquee marked 'St John's Ambulance'.

The nurse looked quite startled. She did not seem to have many customers, and agreed that my condition permitted me to use her facilities. She led me through an area earmarked for a field hospital, to use the tiny throne and washstand tucked away at one end.

"I see you're expecting."

"Yup, this one's going to be a Greek."

In the mirror I saw her gulp. Nonchalantly I added, "I already have two Cypriots and a Saudi at home," then airily exited the tent aware of her open-mouthed expression. On the way home I recounted this conversation to Oliver.

"I don't think I look like an international call girl, do I?"

"Poor woman," Oliver said. "You might have explained what you were talking about."

After returning to Athens, I checked into the posh clinic where our fourth child was due to be born.

"We don't encourage husbands to be present," said the Greek doctor, "but as you are British I'll allow him to stay upstairs with you until we get to the point of delivery."

A few hours later Oliver was ordered out and shown into a waiting room as "it shouldn't take long".

"Mrs Miles, may I invite you with me into the lift?" said the doctor, courteously holding the door.

"What? In this?" I was attired in a delivery gown that brushed my navel and left nothing to the imagination.

"Don't worry."

We entered the public lift, which caused bemusement amongst the genteel Athenian visitors gripping large bouquets. As we plummeted to the basement and the doors slid open, he said, "Welcome to the orchestra".

Female voices wailed "*Iatre, Iatre*" (Doctor! Doctor!), like a Greek Chorus. I was incarcerated in a basement room lined with grey tiles and nothing to read. We had made the cardinal error of not allowing for the Greek sense of time. When after four hours Oliver was led in to admire his daughter he was fairly livid and complained about not having brought his book.

"All that rubbish about it not being a girl," he snapped.

"What is it?" the doctor had quizzed me earlier, standing at a vantage point following the delivery.

"I can't see – is it a boy?" I hedged my bet.

"You foolish woman, anyone can see it is a girl. By the way, what have you got at home?"

It seemed strange to me that he had not taken a family history earlier. "I have three boys."

"Three boys!" The doctor was ecstatic. Forgetting my undignified predicament he ran round the room where a couple of other women were delivering, waving his hands and shouting: "This woman has three boys and now she has a daughter! God be praised."

As we prepared to leave Greece we were aware that serious things were happening elsewhere. In 1979, the Shah was deposed in the Iranian Revolution and Ayatollah Khomeini returned to Tehran from Paris to popular acclaim. One evening Oliver asked if I would accompany him to the Iranian Embassy. We found the Iranian Ambassador sitting in his garden looking grey and morose. He presented the pitiful sight of a man contemplating his own execution and wanted to explore with Oliver the possibility of moving to London. I am afraid I have no idea what happened to him, but I fear the worst.

Soon after we got home to Hampshire we were visited by Moussa Kilani, an old friend of Oliver's, who had been the Jordanian Ambassador to Bahrain. The Iranian Revolution had occurred while he held that post and he, the Saudi, and Iranian Ambassadors – conscious that they represented politically vulnerable countries – pledged to care for one another's family if anything should befall them. Sadly, Moussa told us that he now had an Iranian daughter.

We left Greece at Easter 1980 after a tour of only 30 months. Not knowing that we would return to Athens in a few years' time, I was delighted to have a living souvenir – our daughter Lucy.

She grew up not only speaking Greek and loving the country as much as I did, but believing she was indeed Greek. As we showed our passports at the airport, there was an archetypal Greek moment. We had diplomatic status, so it was unusual to be detained. The official could not understand how we had entered the country as a family of five but he kept counting six. Oliver was not helping, perhaps because he was 'leave happy'. He kept raising his hands to the sky and proclaiming things like "God's blessing" or "It's a miracle" which baffled the passport officer even more. Finally he understood, and we were allowed onto the plane.

The next four years were among the happiest of my life, marred only by the death of my father. Four years of being me, in my own home and finding a job as a social worker at last. But time passed too quickly and with a mixture of apprehension and curiosity, we awaited a decree from Personnel Department as they decided where Oliver should be sent next.

To his delight Oliver was appointed British Ambassador to Libya. Moving from Grade Four is a great moment for any diplomat, because you have achieved the goal of your own Embassy.

Before we left England we had to 'Kiss Hands' with the Queen. This is an ancient and peculiarly British affair, and nowadays no kissing is involved. But when any newly appointed Head of Mission arrives in post he has to present his credentials, given to him by his own Head of State, to the Head of State of the country to which he is appointed. Until the new envoy has done this he cannot operate as an Ambassador.

On appointment, a British Ambassador also receives a beautifully inscribed document – called a Commission – which carries the Royal seal and the signatures of both the Monarch and the Foreign Secretary. This confirms that the Queen has invested authority in him to act as her representative abroad. The wording is wonderfully archaic, beginning: 'To All and Singular to whom these Presents shall come. Greeting! Whereas it appears to Us expedient to nominate some Person of approved Wisdom, Loyalty, Diligence and Circumspection to represent Us in the character of our Ambassador Extraordinary and Plenipotentiary to ...'

A dashing equerry in military uniform escorted us through the palace's huge crimson-carpeted rooms lined with cabinets containing Meissen porcelain and hung with oil paintings, until we reached an antechamber where we were met by a Lady-in-Waiting. A bit of inconsequential conversation ensued until we were told to stand on a mat facing tall, wooden double doors. When they opened we had to bow or curtsy, then walk forward to shake hands and again bow or curtsy to the Queen.

A diminutive figure, she was standing smiling in the middle of the formal sitting room where much State business is conducted. Nobody else is ever present at this ceremony since it is a confidential exchange. She invites her envoy to sit down and discuss the current politics of the country he is heading for, what he anticipates is going to happen during his time there and what he hopes to achieve in terms of British interests. If the Queen has plans to travel there or has any special knowledge of the country she might talk about that, but there are no rules. In effect she bids him farewell with instructions as to the mission ahead.

The written Commission puts it this way: 'Giving and Granting to him in that character all Power and Authority to do and perform proper acts, matters and things which may be desirable or necessary for the promotion of relations and friendship, good understanding and harmonious intercourse between Our Realm and the Socialist People's Libyan Arab Jamahiriya ...' or whatever the post might be.

Oliver could not present credentials in Libya because Colonel Gaddafi claimed there was no Head of State in the Jamahiriya. He simply handed his papers to the Libyan Foreign Minister instead. When he later became ambassador to Luxembourg there was more pomp and circumstance attached to the presentation ceremony. I was instructed to wear a challenging combination of full-length evening dress and hat at 11am to meet the Grand Duke. He is related to our Royal family and as Colonel of the Irish Guards takes part in Trooping the Colour.

The demanding dress code defeated me so I uncharacteristically withdrew with 'diplomatic flu' and missed seeing Oliver resplendent in gold-braided diplomatic uniform, including sword and ostrich-feathered hat, presenting his credentials. I also missed the ceremony when he became ambassador to Greece because it all happened while I was still in England preparing to leave.

Before we left for Libya, the Queen asked me sympathetically about the preparations needed for Tripoli. I could only blurt out that they were 'maniacal'. I could not begin to describe the effort and imagination required in amassing the tons of goods prior to our departure and I did not suppose she would find it very interesting even if she understood what I was going on about. When we met again before going to Luxembourg, the Queen asked how Libya had been. I tried to tell her about the scarcity and price of fresh milk: "A pound a pint, Ma'am". She looked totally baffled, but afterwards Oliver consoled me, "She's a farmer so she only thinks in herds".

I felt very inhibited about what I should say to the Queen. As both Luxembourg and Greece have connections with the British Royal Family she had more to say about these countries but I still found it difficult to have a meaningful conversation. Fortunately, the Queen is more interested in her representative than in his wife, so most of the discussion was between her and Oliver and that seemed to flow.

Over the years, we received several invitations to the palace. On one occasion Oliver was presented with an honour, a CMG (Companion of the Order of St Michael and St George). While Tom, Hugh and I sat in the ballroom awaiting her Majesty's arrival, Tom surveyed the audience and whispered to me, "Who do you suppose all these women are?" Without missing a beat I replied, "Dunno, but in a minute they'll all be Ladies".

We also attended the summer garden parties and the annual diplomatic reception when the entire London Diplomatic Corps lines up according to precedence (depending on how long they have served in London). The Royal family, led by the Queen, goes round the room speaking to each Ambassador and High Commissioner, who introduces senior members of his staff. The rest of us sit on the banked benches of the ballroom enjoying the Guards' band and eyeing the guests. Everyone dresses to the nines, although I noticed that many of the British diplomatic wives had chosen their footwear for comfort rather than style: flip-flops and Dr Scholl's sandals could be glimpsed under ball dresses.

When the Royal Family disappears, the Beefeaters line up to corral everyone into various rooms for the buffet. The FCO Permanent Under-Secretary once tried to duck through them, gripping my elbow. Their halberds came down with a loud clash, and they were not laughing. But it is remarkable how quickly any restraint disappears at the buffet and the once-elegant crowd dissolves into a bun fight. And when a snack is finally grabbed – as was pointed out to me by a Canadian Military Attaché – there is something rather comic about eating a sausage on a stick underneath the canopy that hangs above the throne.

LIBYA: THE CALM BEFORE THE STORM

Before we left England for Libya we were asked to meet the Government Architects' Department to discuss refurbishing the Residence. They reminded me of the obsequious tailors in *The Emperor's New Clothes* as they flattered and cajoled us with lavish plans for woven carpets with patterned borders, luscious silk curtains with rosette-studded pelmets, and, rather strangely, thick tweed upholstered dining chairs. Then they stood back for our acquiescence.

"I'm afraid I consider this rather a waste of taxpayers' money," I said.

"You don't understand," they protested. "We've saved by not spending anything on the servants' quarters."

"And where are they?" enquired Oliver with a glint in his eye.

"In the basement."

"Any air conditioning?"

"Well, er, not exactly."

"And all this refurbishment will be quite disruptive?"

"Not at all. We visit regularly to manage the project."

"That's fine," said Oliver. "You come and visit us and stay in the servants' quarters."

We never heard another squeak from them. In some ways this was a pity, as the frequently flooded drawing room ceiling hung down in a threatening manner and really did need repair.

There was some argument as to how much Gaddafi had actually achieved for the Libyan people, and how much of the groundwork had been laid by his predecessor, King Idris. The oil wealth had allowed the establishment of a Welfare State: free health, schooling and social security benefits. It was rare to see a shoeless beggar, and the children, though scruffy, were reasonably dressed. Occasionally I recognised clothes from Marks & Spencer, because many Libyans travelled abroad to shop. They seemed well fed. Poverty-related eye disease was evident among the older generation (possibly including Gaddafi: we heard he was attended by a British ophthalmologist), but had been virtually eradicated among the young.

The city of Tripoli was undergoing major restructuring when we arrived in 1984. There was a vast Ring Road project with dozens of flyovers, and new roads slashed their way through older suburbs. Much of the population was moving to high-rise blocks. Nobody lived in cardboard boxes or oil drums as we had seen in Saudi Arabia. Thought had even been given to a Planetarium, and we were told that the Museum, which held jumbled-up dusty curiosities like two-headed stuffed goats alongside stunning mosaics, was going to be made into one of the world's finest. The Hotel Kabir's exterior was a showpiece; its wedding-cake magnificence bordered the wide-open space of Green Square, an elegant adjunct to other waterfront buildings.

From previous posts, I had become wised up to potential food shortages. But I knew Colonel Gaddafi, in accordance with his Third Way policy, had swept away all the shops, replacing them with half a dozen huge warehouses severely bereft of goods. So before we left England, I stocked up on everything I could think of. This included a second-hand flute for Oliver, to give him a new hobby. I bought a pamphlet on keeping chickens; compost fertilised with mushroom spores; and dozens of kilos of chocolates which went straight into the freezer. I failed to find a map of Libya or any useful book about the country.

I cannot begin to describe the difficulty of guessing the sizes of four pairs of feet in six months' time, or persuading my doctor to let me have some antibiotic eye drops. "Old Mother Hubbard" he remarked obliquely, as he wrote a list of suggestions for the medicine chest. I also had to estimate how we would fill our spare time, of which I anticipated lots, since Gaddafi had closed down all cafés, cinemas and every other possible source of entertainment, leaving open only a few churches. We set off from home with so much overweight baggage we were penalised to the tune of £800.

Tearing up our settled lives in England had been distressing. Our two eldest sons, dayboys at a prep school, became boarders. Our house had to be made ready for tenants: emptied of everything except the barest essentials, which entailed sifting through and discarding possessions accumulated over four years at home, plus the tedious job of compiling an inventory.

We had acquired a Battersea Dogs' Home dog, a hirsute female terrier with an absentminded demeanour, called Hattie. We sent her on ahead (she didn't seem to mind). Oliver also set off before us, driving our new car. He went overland to Libya, dodging a bomb in Marseilles and reaching Tunisia just as bread riots erupted and arrived in Tripoli the picture of a North African corsair, having walked into a plate-glass door in a garage and giving himself a black eye.

So I was left to pack up the house and the four children. On the day of departure we were up at crack of dawn to jump into a taxi on a freezing January day. Arriving in Tripoli, Hugh, Lucy and I were delighted to be reunited with Oliver but terribly sad about leaving the other two small boys behind. We found Hattie pottering round the two-acre garden. The weather in Libya in January was no warmer than on a nice June day at home so my concern about her capacity to survive in the heat had not yet been tested.

We had barely unpacked before several staff members complained to me about the poor medical facilities. I was worried about the brackish water, which was all there was to drink, so I wrote at once to the Foreign Office medical adviser.

Naturally he did not reply. But quite unexpectedly, a couple of months into our posting he altered his travel plans and did come to Tripoli. I handed him a cup of tea made with the brackish water and he choked on it.

This gave me the perfect opportunity to lecture him on our plight. He agreed that the water quality was sub-standard but nothing was done while we were there. However he was unequivocal about the poor state of our living conditions and the lack of medical care for Embassy staff, which made me worry what we might do in the case of serious illness or accident. To quote from his subsequent report:

"I would comment on the state of the kitchens. Through no fault of the staff the standard of cleanliness is below an acceptable level. Rusting cupboards, inadequate lighting, probably dangerous electric wiring and a non-functioning gas cooker which needs commercial cleaning as well as extensive repair before it can be used would in my opinion mean that this kitchen would be closed by a Health Inspector should it be in a British hotel …"

Regarding the medical care:
"… The London-trained GP asks all his patients to undress even if they have only sprained an ankle. This habit had already excited some comment among the staff and confidence was not enhanced when it was found that this doctor had been practising when struck off by the General Medical Council …"

He went on to comment on the poor hospital provision. "This would appear to be a lavishly over-equipped hospital. Much of the equipment appeared to be in cardboard boxes still … the technical expertise was probably not there to back it up. If machinery went wrong it would appear that repairs are impossible …" Followed by: "The laboratory had adequate equipment but a great deal of it was not working and the technician who was looking at the blood slides etc was smoking at the same time …"

Oliver spoke fluent Arabic, and I could manage a smattering, but Libyans were shy of being seen as friendly to Westerners. Oliver managed to establish good working relationships with many officials, and our hope was that we would break through the barrier of suspicion and distrust and make some real Libyan friends. Sadly, by the time we left we could still only count them on the fingers of one hand.

One friend was a farmer called Said who lived outside Tripoli and who for some years had hospitably entertained members of the Embassy. He used to deliver sacks of oranges stealthily by night, leaving them on our doorstep. The fact that he visited the Residence at all was remarkable, as everyone assumed that visitors to embassies were constantly monitored by the Libyan security services. One day he walked into my sitting room and said, "This is the first time I have ever set foot in a British Embassy house." It was a great compliment. He had taken a risk with his personal safety.

Hugh's teacher, Sylvia Howard and her husband, Brian, an academic vet, introduced us to Misbah, a student at Tripoli University. His jolly relatives, Nadia and Abdu, entertained us in Libyan style both in Tripoli and in the country. On one occasion we all set off to visit Misbah's family's farm. We debated whether we should take alcohol. "Abdu can't drink in front of his father," Brian said. Oliver felt it was dangerous to establish a precedent and if we were caught carrying alcohol around, we would be in trouble. But when Misbah met us half way to the house he delicately indicated that British guests were expected to provide alcohol. It was too far to go back to the Residence. The Howards' house was closer so we called in there. They warned us that they only had home-brewed beer, which they said was rather treacly.

We reached the farm and sat for some time admiring the family photos and sipping sweet, cool almond juice.

Then we looked round the garden. The swimming pool had been cemented over so that it was now a vast underground cistern. I was terrified that one of the children, roller skating on this makeshift playground, would impale himself on the rusty reinforcements sticking up from the concrete. Tin cans and old shoes lay in the grass so the garden was not immediately prepossessing.

We perched on a rickety mustard-yellow sofa on a shady terrace and waited while two sheep were slaughtered. The conversation became desultory. Finally, Brian jumped up and announced that he was going to inspect the cow's teeth. All the men traipsed after him, hoping it was a euphemism, only to find that, being a vet, he was as good as his word. We were growing hungry. A smallish barbecue was lit and some entrails, still warm, tossed on it.

Abdu's father took me for a turn round the garden. "All we need to complete this party is a nice bottle of whisky," he mused, leaning on a stone wall.

I sighed sympathetically. I felt awful that we had not taken the risk of bringing some with us. After a protracted wait, the first course was served: lettuce and fennel with a squeeze of lemon and lurking beneath, a half-baked piece of gut or liver. To my relief, the children were so hungry they gobbled it up without a murmur. Then Misbah, adopting the role of host, sat cross-legged on the cement cistern with two tin teapots. He poured a sweetened dark brown liquid from one to the other, brewing it up intermittently on a camp stove till the result was to his satisfaction. He poured us many rounds of the thick, sweet, mint-flavoured tea served in thimble-sized cups.

Possibly because of its inferior quality Brian never offered his home-made brew. There being nothing else to do we walked round the garden again, where a group of youths were slapping wet sand on the outside of an old clay oven. Abdu explained that the meat would cook slowly and be ready to eat when the sand had completely dried.

"And how long might that take?" I enquired as politely as possible.

"Only about an hour or so. Come and meet my brothers." Abdu indicated the youths. There were eight in the family: all were present with their wives and children. One had become engaged the previous day, so the women's hands were patterned with henna.

"Have you met your future wife?" I asked him.

"Of course. There are no restrictions on us. I can even bring her here alone in the car." That was more liberal than in other Muslim countries.

He pointed out his aged aunt squatting on the ground. She grinned at me toothlessly. Her breasts flapped loosely as she vigorously scrubbed two charred sheep heads with soap powder and what looked like a square of tulle, in dirty water swilling round an upturned dustbin lid. I eyed them dubiously.

"Don't you eat brains?" asked Abdu solicitously.

"Well, I won't now I've seen the expression on that sheep's face."

Thankfully, we were never offered any. If I had shown any enthusiasm we would, naturally, have been invited to share. With some trepidation we had brought our camera along. Photography was not encouraged in Libya. Many Arabs, especially the older generation, remain fearful that it will inflict the evil eye. So I was quite surprised when Abdu encouraged me to stand next to his aged aunt for a snap. What a contrast: she wizened and tiny in a long striped purple-and-yellow garment and me buxom in my denim dress. In a corner of the photograph could be seen a grinning sheep's skull.

We did eventually get fed and drove back to Tripoli planning to return the hospitality. Abdu had made it clear that he was not intimidated by the regime and was ready to drive openly to our house at any time. Alas, it was not to be.

There was not a lot to do in Libya. Having visited the wonderful Roman sites at Sabratha several times and Leptis Magna once, I began to wonder how I might fill the impending three years. Most days, like the rest of the population, I drove around Tripoli searching for food in one of the five supermarkets. Arriving at a litter-strewn parking lot I would join the group of white-cloth covered Libyan women waiting for the shop to open. They held their head-covering between their teeth, peering at me out of their one uncovered eye. At last a little old man removed the splintery plank that held the door fast and we shuffled forward into the vast shop.

There were rows of Italian detergents and soap, piles of canned tomato paste, chick peas and battered cardboard packets from which salt was oozing, as well as rows of empty freezer cabinets. I supposed these were for rare appearances of butter and milk. After I had drunk some fresh milk, Brian told me not to do so again as it was contaminated with brucellosis. In the aisle were 50-kilo sacks leaking Cuban sugar, and bags of Italian flour too heavy to move. And that was all.

The vegetable market with its dazzling produce was a big contrast. A kilo of anything cost one dinar (£2.50), except for aubergines or peppers rated at two dinars. The only fruit we ever saw were oranges, and dates compressed into 'cakes'. These were full of gritty sand and, according to Abdullah – our 'butler' from Niger – other horrors, so he stopped me from buying them. On Fridays when livestock was being sold you would see pairs of camels sitting regally in the back of Japanese pick-ups chewing the cud with a supercilious expression. Camels cost 500 dinars apiece, which equated to about £1200 sterling.

There were live chickens, turkeys and guinea fowl all with their legs tied together so that they spilt over the ground in feathery bundles. There were enormous bulls insecurely tethered with parcel string. Small boys chased and caught sheep and goats by a single back leg while a Libyan bagpiper droned a monotonous three-toned tune from an instrument concocted of two cows' horns and an udder. The days passed uneventfully and I was happy when Joe and Tom flew out from their boarding schools in England to join us for the Easter holidays. But the dull monotony of life in Tripoli had lulled me into a sense of false security.

EMBASSY UNDER SIEGE

There were numerous Libyans living in the UK who hated Gaddafi and his regime. Occasionally Gaddafi would send a hit squad to assassinate a few of these 'stray dogs', and one of Oliver's missions was to dissuade the regime from using our country for their murderous sorties. On 17 April 1984 some of these dissidents organised a political demonstration opposite the People's Bureau (the Libyan Embassy), on the corner of St James's Square in London. Freedom to protest is upheld in Great Britain and there was no reason to stop it. The police, as always on such occasions, were present.

That morning, a young constable named Yvonne Fletcher took up her position facing the Libyan demonstrators, with her back to the building. Suddenly, shots rang out from the People's Bureau, aimed at the protesters. WPC Fletcher was hit in the back, stomach and leg. She died from her injuries.

WPC Fletcher's death was to have unprecedented consequences for us. After only four months, our time was up. This is an edited version of the account that I wrote at the time of our nine-day siege and evacuation of Libya. It began in the early hours of Wednesday, 17 April 1984.

We had stayed out later than usual at a dinner at the Spanish Embassy and when we arrived home the phone was ringing. It was Ian Cooling, the Head of Chancery.

"But it's one o'clock in the morning," I heard Oliver say. "Now? They must be mad."

"Shall I come with you?" I asked.

"No, it's only the Foreign Liaison Bureau, that building on the corner. I'll be back in five minutes."

He was.

"I saw a new man – Hafiana. It's difficult to know how much importance to attach to what he said but there's going to be a demonstration outside the People's Bureau in London tomorrow and they want us to stop it. There are often demonstrations; they're quite lawful. I don't know why he's in such a flap about this one, but I'll send a telegram to London, anyway."

The next morning started quite normally. I took Hugh and Lucy to school, which gave me a couple of hours before they needed collecting. I spent the time before my piano lesson walking along the beach buying the catch from any fisherman I could find. At lunchtime, Abdullah, our 'butler', was listening to the news on a French radio station. He tried to explain in his Franco-Arabic-Hausa patois that something had happened, but I could not understand. Oliver dashed in and out again. He had been to the Foreign Liaison Bureau a second time. "No time to explain, but please cancel the school committee meeting this afternoon and my first flute lesson, dammit …"

At 3.30pm Norah, the wife of the Brazilian Ambassador, called.

"I should shut those gates of yours," she said tersely. "Good luck."

I thought to myself, "The trouble with foreigners is that they get windy too easily." Shutting the gates would signal some unease to the outside world. In any case the back wall was so low that little boys were able to shin over it to retrieve their footballs, so we left the gates open and felt quite secure.

Barbara Cooling drove up. The Cooling family had been looking for somewhere to live ever since their arrival 15 months earlier. They had finally found a large house rather far from the Embassy, but their heavy baggage was still stacked in our garage.

"Something funny is happening at the Embassy," she said. "I went to get my meat out of the freezer in the basement but I couldn't get in." I had gleaned from Oliver that something was wrong, but I had no facts. Lack of communication was a huge issue in Libya, where few people had telephones. But earlier a man had phoned me to say that as he and his wife were returning to England, they intended to drop off their pet rabbit at the Residence that afternoon.

"Who else is going to look after it?" he had demanded. "My wife is a great animal lover and she rescued Honeybun off the butcher's slab – just couldn't bear seeing her slaughtered." He left no name or contact details and delivered Honeybun surreptitiously while Barbara and I were chatting. The rabbit turned out to be an enormous and extremely vicious animal.

During the next few days I wanted to take Honeybun to Said's farm but we were forbidden to leave Tripoli. If only Honeybun and our dog Hattie had gone to the farm, our life would have been a great deal quieter after we left Libya.

The Residence was in the bottom two floors of an enormous house that Mussolini's top admiral had built for his personal use. The 70-foot salon took up a small proportion of the ground floor, the grand piano scarcely visible in a far corner. Its size and inefficient layout required staff but these were hard to find: no Libyan wanted to be a servant, as they were 'partners, not wage earners' (as banners at the airport declared). Fortunately I had help – we had brought Ben and Marilyn, a Filipino couple, and the cook Sarah, from England, to join Abdullah in running the house.

When Barbara left, the phone rang: it was Fiona Davies, the wife of the Administration Officer. She and all the other families lived about five miles away from us in 'GP' – Georgimpopuli or, as the Libyans call it, Andalus. Most of the foreign schools were situated there.

"Have you got any – er – 'visitors' hanging round your house?" Fiona used heavy emphasis. "I can't get through to Paul and I do feel a bit vulnerable out here alone with two small kids and these ruffians outside." I promised to try the Embassy and phone her back.

I had a quick look out of the front door and to my amazement saw about half a dozen Libyan policemen and a van blocking my gateway.

I marched down the drive. "What is this?"

A little man in a greasy uniform with pips on his shoulder said, "All right, lady. All right."

I said, "My friend in GP very worried. Men at house. You go there, Colonel."

He giggled. "Me Captain here, me no Andalus."

"Never mind, Colonel, you phone police Andalus."

I escorted him into the hall and he spent a while spitting into the telephone, finally saying:

"OK, Andalus police look Embassy houses. Like British. Me Royal Air Force 29 years."

He went back to his post and I sent some tea out for him. I went to phone Oliver and got through after several attempts.

"We've got the police outside. Barbara's gone home after failing to get into the Office – tell Ian. Fiona has some unsavoury types who won't let her go out of her gate. What on earth's happening?"

"A policewoman has been shot dead in London. There was machine gunfire from inside the People's Bureau. Stay put, and tell the other wives not to leave their homes under any circumstances."

Tim Nugent, a good-looking Canadian ex-clown and music teacher from the Oil School, appeared on his mono-cycle. Tuesday night was music night in the Residence and he was the choir conductor.

"Sure I got in, no problem." He knew more than me. "I don't expect there will be many people coming tonight if they've heard the news: a policewoman killed, 11 anti-Gaddafi protesters injured and the police have ringed the People's Bureau in St James' Square. I guess this is sort of retaliation."

I went to phone the wives and all were in reasonable shape. Fiona had found a helpful male British neighbour so felt less vulnerable. Rosemary Anderson, the Consul's wife, had a couple of Revolutionary Committee characters, or possibly secret police, hanging around. She said she felt reasonably safe with a teenage stepdaughter and a nanny for her two-month-old baby. Barbara Cooling was unpacking as there had been a time lag in the news reaching her.

"If you have any trouble," I said, "get onto Mujib Rahman, the Bangladeshi Ambassador. He lives opposite you. He's fit and athletic, I know he'd come over."

Sue Pigott was the only one not to answer the phone. No one had heard from her since earlier in the day.

I phoned Oliver.

"Tell the husbands to ring their wives and let them know what's happening. They've got guards on their gates and are a bit scared. I can't raise Sue. Keep someone on the switchboard all the time. I've asked our policeman to get some police active in GP. He says he has, but no one has uniformed men at their gate except me."

Hastily, he replied, "We've got most of the Embassy children in the Office with us. I'm talking to the Libyans and to London. Tell Sarah if she goes out with her boyfriend she'll probably be arrested."

I went to the gates to retrieve the gold-rimmed porcelain tea set in which Ben had served tea to our guards. David Parry arrived to sing.

"The Embassy is surrounded by police," he said.

"Five minutes, five minutes." The police bunched their fingers and thumb into a tulip shape, indicating the amount of time my visitors could stay.

For three hours we sang, stopping once because the incongruity of the situation hit us and we dissolved into hysterical laughter. We stopped again to listen to the BBC World Service news and to try to fit a coat hanger into the back of the primitive TV set, which was incapable of picking up the English-language Libyan channel. So we watched the Libyan Arabic Channel and could tell from the pictures that the Libyans had not announced the news from London.

Then BBC Scotland rang to ask if they could interview me. I told them that the British community was very calm and in fact, at that very moment, engaged in singing madrigals.

"You're what?" said the Scottish voice incredulously.

The interview concluded and the singers started to leave.

"… And when you do go out for God's sake keep your mouths shut and not just because of the alcohol …" said someone.

The metal gates clanged together and I returned to the silent house. The phone rang. It was the Spanish Ambassador.

"Hi, Carlos."

"Look Julia, are you all right?"

"I'm carrying on as normal but Oliver isn't home and I find it very difficult to get through to the Embassy by phone."

"I fear very much for your Embassy building; they'll burn it tomorrow for sure. But don't worry; Oliver will be safe. They always give warnings."

I felt chilled and went to bed to sleep fitfully for a couple of hours. I kept thinking how lucky it was that this crisis had arisen during the school holidays. At least all the children and I were together. Oliver had been in tight spots before and was probably enjoying negotiating – after all, conflict resolution is a principal aim of diplomacy. I knew his reputation among the Libyans was high, although we had lived in the country for less than four months. I was sure he would come through all right and I was able to comfort Joe when he came into my room in the small hours.

At 8am I phoned the Office. "British Embassy," an exhausted voice answered.

"Can I speak to Oliver please?"

There was a 'click' and the line went dead. I tried several more times. There was no doubt that our home phone line had been deliberately cut.

The house, large and eerie at the best of times, suddenly seemed like a marble mausoleum. Someone had mentioned that our radio was computer programmed but I had absolutely no idea how to work it. I realised to my horror that without it we were completely cut off from the outside world.

So we gravitated to Lucy's bedroom. She had chicken pox so we kept her company by sorting jigsaws on the floor. Abdullah remained *blasé*, having been through this sort of political upheaval before. It occurred to me that I should try to send a note to the Embassy, together with Oliver's flute and some clean shirts. There were three occupied staff flats in the Embassy so I knew that the Security Officers' wives would look after whoever was stuck in there.

"Abdullah," I yelled.

"Hallooooah."

"What happened in 1980 when the Ambassador suddenly left Libya? Did they cut the telephone?" We spoke in Franglais.

"It's first thing they do. They like children." He gave a big holler and swayed around on his double-jointed hips. Clearly the sirens screaming up and down the road, which sounded ominous to me, did not worry him. I kept thinking of the Spanish Ambassador's warning and thought I might be able to see a pall of smoke but we were too far away.

"Forty policeman round house today. I got pass to go out. I counted them."

"In that case, please see if you can get this bag and letter into the Office. It is totally innocent if they want to search it." I hoped they wouldn't mistake the flute for a weapon.

Abdullah had a well-developed sense of conspiracy, for he put the letter down the back of his shirt, seized the bag and rolled off in his loose-limbed way towards the gate. Twenty minutes later he was back, crestfallen.

"No open door." The letter had slipped so far down that he had to retire modestly to retrieve it. So we had to carry on as normal, whatever that meant in this strange situation.

I practised the Chopin mazurka for my next piano lesson but was interrupted by the arrival of Isobel and Peta, friends from the British community.

"We just walked in. The guards forbade the car but they didn't stop us. We came to see if you were all right."

I felt pleased that someone had witnessed that we were still alive. Later I heard that many kind people had tried to visit me but were turned away. Isobel and Peta only had the inevitable five minutes, so I tried to think quickly.

"Take some money and phone my mother in England. Tell her not to worry. And can you phone the Embassy and tell them we're completely cut off; they probably haven't realised. And please, come again."

"We didn't know what to bring you but I've got a full gas cylinder in the car, if you want.

"Isobel, you are a wonder! We may be stuck for days so yes, please ..."

I remembered the Iranian siege when American diplomats had been held for over a year. One of the US Embassy wives in Athens had described her experience during that siege and I remembered her saying the two things you should take in an emergency were your passport and your family photo album. We had just finished lunch when Sarah, the cook, rushed in.

"Abdullah remembered the other phone!"

"What other phone?"

"In the Gents apparently – you know, the changing rooms behind the swimming pool. It's got a lock on it but we can break that."

Joe ran off to look for a jemmy.

We all made for the outbuilding, discreetly tucked behind the swimming pool. There was a phone and it did have a lock. We clustered round as Joe tried to prise it off. Abdullah kept apologising for not having thought of it before.

"Ambassador come home! Look."

There stood Oliver with Carsten Pigott.

I started gabbling. "Marvellous to see you ... what's happening? We are cut off from the outside world ... nothing works ... bet you it's a breach of Human Rights ..."

"Look, we've got five minutes."

"Not you, too ..."

"Carsten's being my driver. I'm going to the Foreign Liaison Bureau. I must say hello to the kids and get my flute ..."

"Daddy, Daddy ..."

"Carsten, what happened to Sue? I couldn't get hold of her last night."

"Oh, she's fine. She was watching a video, feet up, oblivious." He scraped the bowl of his pipe. "She'd just left the phone off the hook, that was all."

Oliver took hold of my arm. "Can I have a quick word in private?" We moved out of earshot. "Look, we may be going to break off diplomatic relations, we must be prepared for that. Don't breathe a word. The women and children may be let out before the staff."

"I reckon the wives scattered all round town are in a really difficult position. At least you men in the Office have each other for moral support and you are in touch with London. We don't even have a working radio now. Oh, by the way: I was interviewed by BBC Scotland last night. Did you hear me? "

"No – you must tell me about it sometime. Everyone is OK. All the men are in touch with their wives and it's turning into a sort of party in the Office. We were going to watch the film *Escape from New York* last night, but were too busy. Some are playing snooker and darts or even cricket in the corridors. And we are all being well looked after. Must go and see Treiki – you know – Foreign Minister. I'll complain to him about your phone."

I felt much cheered by this visit and since Carsten had wrenched off the lock, I thought I should see whether the phone worked. I dialled my mother's number and to my astonishment, the call went through.

"Sorry," she kept saying. "To whom I am speaking?"

It was infuriating, but I took a deep breath and told her again.

"Glad you rang," she said. "I've been wondering whether you got the sunhats."

Oh well, all was evidently fine at her end.

The house phone rang! Good old Oliver had got them to plug it back in. A foreign correspondent in Rome. It was terribly comforting to talk to another adult. Little did I know that a Press assault had begun.

ITN rang: a live interview. Could I hold on?

"Look, I'm doing 'dressing Teddy,'" I said, as Lucy wailed for attention.

Sloane Ranger voice: "Sounds really quite normal out there. Here's Leonard Parkin; remember this is live."

"Hello, Mrs Miles. Where are you now?"

"Sitting on the bed on the first floor of the Residence." I remembered not to mention Teddy.

"Where in relation to the Embassy building are you?"

"About a quarter of a mile down the road."

He relaxed and we chatted happily.

Sloane Ranger came back on: "That was fine, Mrs Miles. Thank you."

"Have you got a picture to go with this interview?" I asked.

"Oh yes, we've got a very nice picture."

"I wonder where you got it from."

Oliver had had special Press photos taken in London for just such an eventuality. The Foreign Office had also given him training for Press interviews, although it was quite unusual for diplomatic staff to speak out. For a wife to do so was pretty unprecedented. I was probably taking a risk with Oliver's career talking openly like this, but I really did not care.

"It's an aerial photo of Tripoli. Goodbye."

At no time during this crisis did anybody in the Foreign Office bother to call to see how we or any other Embassy family were faring. When challenged, the FCO Under-Secretary gave the breathtaking excuse that they did not think they could dial direct. Since an ex-social work client in Basingstoke phoned me as soon as the crisis started, this was a pretty lame excuse. It suited me not to be gagged by the Foreign Office, but I bet they were in a state of impotent fury every time I surfaced in the media – which was often.

I phoned round all the wives, who sounded cheerful but bored of being locked in, especially with young children. Most were short of sleep but morale was high. All afternoon my phone rang, with the Press calling from the US, Canada, Italy, France, Yugoslavia. I was up to my knees in the pond rescuing drowning ladybirds with Lucy but I was sure that I had a duty to keep the world informed. Besides, it was pretty therapeutic for me to offload.

"Don't like soldiers," protested Lucy. I had barely noticed that some of our guards were now military. They didn't bother us except that we were still not allowed out. I looked over the wall. Darwin, the gardener's boy, was trying to come in to work. He was being shouldered towards a truck by a mean-looking, cross-eyed soldier.

"Leave him alone," I cried, running through the gate. Cross Eyes looked taken aback, but then resumed shoving.

"I'll come tomorrow," said Darwin and made off as fast as he could. We never saw him again.

Later that day, Oliver returned with Carsten only to encounter Cross Eyes bossily strutting around. Oliver's face went pale with anger.

"Do you know who I am?" he asked in Arabic. Cross Eyes pretended not to understand. Oliver thrust his face up close.

"I am the British Ambassador, and this is my house." Cross Eyes looked at him impassively. "Have you not had your instructions that we have freedom of movement? Get in my car please. I will take you to Dr Treiki so that he can spell it out to you. Get in."

Cross Eyes shifted uneasily.

"Right. Then I will go to Dr Treiki and tell him."

Oliver jumped in the car and sped off to the Foreign Liaison Bureau. Cross Eyes spoke rapidly into his radio and then he too disappeared – in the opposite direction. We never had another soldier at the gate, at least not one in uniform.

A little later Oliver reappeared with Carsten and Paul Davies, the Administration Officer, and his replacement, Red

Norton, who had arrived two days earlier. They all smelt but were going home to bath and change now they'd been let out.

"Poor you, Red, it's tough that you and the Sargons have only just arrived, and this has happened. But perhaps it's better not having your family around?"

"Not at all. My wife is dreadfully upset because she can't imagine what it's like out here."

We stood on the terrace drinking whisky as the sun went down. They were all so tired they could hardly speak. As I accompanied them to the guarded gate, I realised I was still clutching a glass of whisky. It was easy to become careless. I fled back to the house.

CONCEALMENT
AND CONFUSION

We fell into bed at 11.30pm. At 1am the phone rang. It was Red. He had sent Martin, a registry clerk – a young bachelor beloved by all, but terribly accident prone – to deliver a telegram to the house. Red had taken the precaution of a prearranged signal in case Martin failed to arrive. It seemed that he had indeed disappeared so frantic alarm bells were ringing.

We went downstairs to find Martin standing on the doorstep looking frail. It transpired that he had ventured out into the night without any form of identification and had been picked up by the police although they had seen him leave the Embassy. His identity card was at the Department of Protocol for renewal and he had not had an opportunity to go home to fetch his passport.

"I hate to say this," stammered Martin, "but my car has broken down and it's blocking your gate. I'm afraid, Ambassador, you won't be able to drive out in the morning."

THURSDAY 18 APRIL

Oliver and I rose early and spent some time unlocking the rusted-up back gate so that he could get to work. We were no longer confined to the house and I was struck by his sudden concern for our safety. The rules of the game were being made up as we went along and it was foolhardy to assume we could move around as normal.

I decided to test my newly regained freedom by going to the market. I don't think I was followed but I did get the distinct impression that as I walked amongst the stalls, the Libyan shoppers nudged each other and looked pointedly in my direction. Nobody said anything or hindered me in any way. On the way home I thought I would drive past the Embassy building to see how things looked. I had expected lots of police, but I was surprised to see busloads of military reinforcements offloading round the back.

On my return, I found the Davies family had arrived at the Residence bringing two children and tennis gear, with two goons in a following car. Red Norton was with them. Soon after Ian Cooling, the Head of Chancery, arrived.

"We've just had the mandatory demonstration outside the Embassy," announced Ian briskly. "Paddy wagon and water cannon drawn up: all very much under control." You could tell he had been a military man despite his foppish hairstyle.

Without asking permission he installed himself in the Residence and took it upon himself not only to answer my phone, but to deal with each call in his own way. Standing right next to him I heard him say, "She's frightfully busy in the kitchen. I'll see if she's able to come to the phone." Then, having counted to 10 and with no reference to me, he said, "No, sorry, she's completely tied up." This continued all day.

I was incensed. To this day I wonder why I failed to challenge Ian's insolence. I think I gave him the benefit of the doubt, persuading myself that the Embassy might be using the Residence as a sort of outpost so that our phone would be available for more important calls than interviews with me. But I did wonder if he had orders from London to stop me speaking to the media. He mentioned (but never showed me) a telegram from the FCO, quoting a very flattering leader about me in the *Evening Standard*, but also instructing him to tell me to shut up. But until somebody told me directly to stop, I was not going to.

I wondered what jurisdiction, if any, the Foreign Office had over me. Oliver never tried to stop me, and perhaps it suited his purposes to have his wife as a sort of unauthorised front, so long as I didn't go over the top and reveal any secrets.

Jeff Asmah, the Ghanaian Ambassador, arrived. I knew Oliver was keen to draw him and the Kuwaiti Ambassador into negotiations as both had influence with the Libyans. It seems that was something we and the other Europeans may have lacked. Jeff was not a career diplomat, but an army officer, tall and handsome. He told me that the Commonwealth should provide solidarity and he would do all he could to help. Then privately, he said I was to tell Oliver that his government was trying to find mediators in New York and London but until the Libyans agreed to this, it had to be kept secret.

"I'll phone Oliver to tell him you're here."

"You'll never get through on the switchboard and Oliver is too busy to speak to you," declared Ian, still commandeering my phone. I gave him a withering look as my call was answered.

Oliver told me that another demonstration would start at 1pm outside the Embassy but he would like to see Jeff, if he would come into the Office. He mentioned there were now two or three American network correspondents in town and this might be the reason for all the demonstrations, which would be thoroughly stage-managed. Libyans, to Gaddafi's chagrin, were by nature too apathetic and lackadaisical to make good revolutionary material, it seemed, and no Libyan demonstration was ever spontaneous.

The demos were often composed of unlikely people like secondary schoolgirls in sailor suits, but on this occasion, as I had witnessed, busloads of army recruits had been delivered to the Embassy. In such a volatile country it was difficult to predict the outcome. Early on in our stay there had been a demonstration outside our Embassy and a petition was passed to Oliver. He could not believe his eyes when he found it was an invitation to tea that afternoon on a nearby farm.

Later, I got a phone call to confirm that the second demonstration had passed off peacefully. Oliver said he particularly had liked the banner which proclaimed: 'Jamahiriya: love it or leave it', which he took to mean 'if you don't like the heat of the kitchen, don't stay.'

It seemed that the moment to torch the Embassy was passing.

That day we gave a farewell lunch to the British Community chaplain, who had come to the end of his time in Tripoli. Afterwards, Fiona and Paul Davies, Red Norton and I played tennis. The Davies were adamant that they would not leave me till Oliver returned. It was good to have company but I also needed time to think. A diversion was provided in the early evening by a continuous stream of wailing fire engines and police cars up and down the coast road. Paul took the boys up onto the roof with binoculars but could not discover the reason for the noise, which continued for five hours.

When the Italian Ambassador phoned that night, I asked if he had been disturbed by the sirens, as he lived just a mile beyond us on the same road. A few days later he told me that he had seen a vast column of thick black smoke to the Southeast, in the direction of the Nuclear Research Station and the main air base. But Abdullah, our butler, assured us it was only a five-storey supermarket on the desert road that had burned. Abdullah was well placed to know: he was the Foreign Minister of Niger's brother and had been called on to join the official delegation during a formal visit by the President of Niger to Libya.

Later that afternoon Red sought me out and whispered conspiratorially:

"I want your passport details and those of the servants."

"I don't know theirs – if I ask them they'll wonder why. You must have their records in the Office."

"It's better we do without. At this stage we don't want any leaks."

"Are we really going?" I was delighted.

"We'll probably drive to Tunisia so that we can get all the cars and most of the luggage out. Oliver will have to drive the Jag. Can you manage your Peugeot?"

The prospect of an Embassy convoy, slowly moving along the potholed coast road with irritable children in the back seat, filled me with dread.

"Of course," I said.

Oliver had missed the monthly European Community Ambassadors' meeting on Wednesday so he invited them to tea on Thursday. They arrived looking so well groomed as they stepped from their official cars that I felt life was almost normal again, and very much at odds with my conversation with Red. I wondered if his passport list was someone's idea of keeping idle hands gainfully employed.

When the Ambassadors moved into the garden for tea, I joined them. They were thoughtful and silent. Did they know a break was imminent, I wondered. Most had had their own difficulties with the Libyans: the French Embassy had been burned down in 1981; the Germans had taken retaliatory action when the Libyans had arrested some of their nationals; the Italians had been the targets of demonstrations often enough, with shots fired into the air outside their Residence. The question was how to deal with a powerful mad minority in a country that meant a lot in terms of trade and was host to vast numbers of expatriates. This was a professional challenge for any diplomat.

That night Oliver told me that London was determined to break off diplomatic relations. A bomb, presumed to be Libyan, had exploded at Heathrow airport, injuring a number of people. It was thought that British public opinion would not tolerate any further violation of their sovereign territory. Since the day of the St James's Square shooting, newspaper articles had unanimously called for a break.

"Can you think of an alternative?" Oliver asked. "It's such a retrograde step and such a pity when I know we are making headway here."

Oliver had used the honeymoon period following our arrival to promote trade and get British prisoners released from jail. It was his first post as Ambassador and I knew he desperately wanted it to continue, especially as he believed that he could make a difference.

"OK – how about a roving Ambassador? I could stay in England and you could fly in and out every month." That would certainly have suited me.

"Hey, I like it. It would maintain a lifeline between the two countries, protect the British community and keep trade at a high level. But it would also show the Libyans our displeasure. I'll try it on London."

FRIDAY 19 APRIL

There were now so many Press people in town that Oliver said it would be a kindness to offer them some hospitality.

"Open house, swimming and refreshments," I heard him tell the first caller. "Any time after 10.30am."

Despite their enthusiasm and gratitude for the invitation, not one Press person arrived. I was practising my mazurka again when Maria Ioannides from Agence France Presse walked in unannounced.

"The others asked permission to leave the hotel. I've been to Libya before and I know the only thing is to keep going until you're stopped."

"Asking permission means a refusal," I said.

"They're all weighed down with cameras so they can't get here easily anyway."

We discussed the situation. Gaddafi had given a television interview to the American network ABC, which Libyan television had shown the previous evening. I had seen it and remarked on his resemblance to a crocodile: the harsh stretched mouth, the cold grey eyes and the way he swayed his head to and fro.

"Yes, he's aged," Maria agreed. "He used to be quite handsome. He looks more pockmarked now. Some say he uses drugs."

I had heard this before but it seemed to me that the Colonel was in full control both of his faculties and his minions.

"American interceptor planes overheard instructions to the People's Bureau ordering them to shoot," she said. This was the first of many conspiracy theories aired about St James Square.

"Even so I can't believe he ordered the policewoman to be killed. What did he hope to achieve?" A pot shot at the Libyan protesters was well within the rules of the game.

"I was so looking forward to Easter," Maria said. "We were to have a reunion in Holland with my sister and now I'm here instead."

The fact that it was Good Friday had completely escaped me. I always thought Easter was a depressing time of year; I wondered if it would be this time.

John Blackstone from CBS appeared: smooth, perfumed. He suggested that the kids and I visit the Hotel Kabir that afternoon. I guessed he would expect me to help him – which was perfectly reasonable, as I had not shrunk from speaking out before.

The Hotel Kabir was thronged by reporters and cameramen, some roped to their sound recordists, which made them like unwieldy trucks on tow. The smoothie interviewers stood behind an interested local crowd and lobbed questions at us.

"Wouldn't it be better in Jamaica?" yelled one.

I had no idea what the point of that question was. It dawned on me how easily one can be ensnared by the Press, and at that time I didn't know whether they were on our side or not.

"Come up and see the footage we've shot so far," said John Blackstone.

The boys and I jumped into the lift. It's quite a shock to see oneself on tape and John only made it worse by commenting: "These cameras make everything look wonderful."

In one respect he was right. The part of Tripoli we lived in, close to the waterfront, still retained several Italian buildings and did indeed look wonderful. Rows of palm trees and elegant fountains (dry, as there was no water) fringed the coast road. Tripoli was the prettiest city I had served in up until then.

It was easy to imagine the place spruced up and cleared of litter so that the white marble frontages looked stylish. Old timers talked wistfully of pre-Revolutionary days with Italian-style street life.

When we re-emerged, someone introduced me to Mohamed, a pale young Libyan from the Information Department who was evidently hard-pressed to keep control of his maverick international press charges. He was supported by a smoother bald-headed guy, much more in the bureaucratic mould. He reinforced Mohamed's line that "of course everyone was free to move around, so long as they go on the bus".

"I don't see any bus," I said to John Blackstone.

After some dancing around – in which my car was loaded and unloaded with camera equipment at least twice – I set off home with the boys and a few cameramen. Only Sarah was around that day as the Muslim servants regularly had Fridays off, and because it was Easter, the Catholic Filipinos were off, too.

"Sarah, please give these gents something to drink." I gave her a knowing look in the direction of the drinks cupboard. "I'm off to fetch the others."

The look of gratitude at my reappearance on the faces of the newspapermen waiting at the hotel suggested they were often victims of unfulfilled promises. Later I discovered that Gaddafi, courting the publicity, had paid for their travel to cover the crisis, and they were technically his guests.

"Of course I wasn't going to leave you stranded," I said. "Where's the famous bus?"

"Do you mind some Libyan journalists?" asked the balding bureaucrat.

I was delighted that they were interested enough to take the unprecedented step of crossing the Embassy threshold.

"OK – after this lot."

As we drove off, fully laden, a thought shot through my head: the first contingent were by now mopping up a bottle of whisky. It was imperative that I got to the house quickly.

"Look chaps," I said. "I'm going to drive like the clappers and you've got to hide every bottle of booze before the Libyans arrive."

They were probably disappointed but to their credit, before I had even stopped the car, there was a frenetic tumbling out of Pressmen and camera crews (fortunately no longer roped together). Within seconds the garden was as irreproachable as a vicar's tea party, just as the first Libyan contingent arrived.

A BBC man came panting up. "Had to wait for visas."

Good old Auntie going by the book. "How British to get the paperwork straight," remarked a snide Yankee voice.

"Have some apple juice."

They eyed it with silent disdain.

"Is your husband around?" This, of course, was their mission.

Just then Oliver walked through the gate. Fifty pairs of feet trampled the turf in his direction. He sat down wearily. The cameras whirred and questions started. They abruptly stopped as the two *muezzins* situated at diagonally opposite points on our boundary began their unsynchronized call to prayer, which we endured five times a day. Once ceased, the questions began again. Mid-interview Lucy, aged four, made her way towards Oliver carefully carrying a glass. Standing full-square in front of the cameras she announced solemnly, "Don't worry Daddy, it's only apple juice."

That moment was witnessed by about 20 million North American viewers. It sent the present company into paroxysms of laughter – apart from the Libyans, who didn't get the joke.

Journalists continued to jam the phones both in the house and at the Office. One question kept coming up: "How are the Libyans taking this?" It was impossible to know. Few Libyans probably had any idea, or interest, in what was happening either on their doorstep or in London. Most were too taken up battling bureaucracy and the daily round of searching for food to pay attention to yet another of Gaddafi's squabbles.

Libyans had little inclination for the politics extolled by Gaddafi's Little Green Book, his 'Third Way', and the policy of 'direct democracy' which he achieved by default. He had found the people sticky in recent months. He lost on the question of women's compulsory military service. Although many 18-year-old girls may have longed for quick emancipation, their traditionalist parents preferred to arrange hasty marriages rather than allow them to be called up. Gaddafi retaliated by closing all the cake shops. Did he think women especially enjoy eating cake or was this to force them to stay home, baking?

Paradoxically, he wanted to close all primary schools as he had concluded that a child's place is with its mother. He also posted an edict to close all barbers' shops: it was fortunate for the Diplomatic Corps that the Belgian Ambassador's driver was in the hairdressing business. Sometimes you didn't know whether to laugh or cry. When Oliver was writing his 'First Impressions Despatch', required by the FCO of all newly arrived Ambassadors, I had a suggestion.

"You should present Libya in the form of *The Wizard of Oz*."

"How do you mean?"

"Well, everything in Oz was green, like here." Green Square was a copy of St Mark's in Venice, but idiosyncratically the Libyans had painted its floor green. "Oz was guarded by green girls and so is Gaddafi, the flags, shutters, car number plates, hoardings – everything is green. Also, take the paranoia of the border witches: Oz and Gaddafi spend a lot of time and trouble eradicating their neighbours – like Chad and Egypt – perhaps even Sudan."

"OK, I get the parallel but Oz himself – is he like Gaddafi?"

"Well, in the final analysis, the Wizard turned out to be a humbug ..."

"Ah, that may be the crucial difference. I don't think Gaddafi is a sham."

Nevertheless, I was gratified to find a direct quote from L. Frank Baum's story in Oliver's final draft to London.

SATURDAY 20 APRIL

The Libyans were getting impatient: negotiations were too slow. I agreed. But Oliver was battling the question of a complete break with my idea of a non-resident Ambassador, for which there was some support.

"Your idea is not a dead duck yet, but I don't think it will win." He didn't yet know that Mrs Thatcher's mind was already made up. There would be nothing short of a total break.

Then the newspapers announced the Libyan bomb at Heathrow.

"British public opinion is not going to tolerate that. I'm afraid that's kissed goodbye to your idea of a non-residential representative."

"Actually I'm more worried about the preparations for the Queen's Birthday Party next Thursday. We've invited 250 people and I have no idea what to do about the catering. Do I buy crates of soft drinks or not?"

"Hold on a couple of days. I don't think we should call it off yet. There are bound to be some developments soon, if only because Parliament is reconvening on Wednesday and ministers will have some answering to do."

As Ramadan fell in June that year we had special dispensation to hold the QBP early. I had slipped in a request that the women helpers at the Embassy library, who worked in the basement of our Residence, should be invited. They deserved a reward for keeping such an important amenity going; as there was no British Council in Tripoli, the library was a vital resource.

The Indian Ambassador had just arrived *en poste* and made his formal introductory call. He reported that Mrs Gandhi, who had recently made a State visit to Libya, had instructed him to be helpful in resolving this dispute.

"I'll be frank," said Oliver. "We're going to break off diplomatic relations."

Mr Atuk looked stunned. "Can't you reconsider it? It's a most retrograde step. What about your expatriate community here?"

"They're a tough lot and know the score," I said.

"Not all of them deserve what they get, like poor old Ledingham." Ledingham was the British Caledonian Airlines manager who had been picked up apparently at random at the beginning of this crisis and was being held as a hostage in jail.

This pointless exercise was typical of the arbitrary harassment the Libyan government meted out under pressure.

I tried to clean out the swimming pool as I thought it might provide some cheer to those working long hours in the cooped-up Office. A replacement vacuum cleaner hose had never materialised in the diplomatic bag, so Paul and I became increasingly ingenious, but unsuccessful, in our efforts to make the old one work so the water still looked like khaki brown soup.

Sue Pigott was full of beans when she rang me later that day.

"Julia Burton has phoned from England." The Burtons were number two in the Embassy hierarchy but had gone on leave a week after our arrival, so we hardly knew them. Somebody had to do their packing. "She's asked me to deal with her cats, and I've got to find the David Roberts' prints and her jewellery. This is going to be fun."

SATURDAY NIGHT, 20 APRIL

No longer was there any doubt about our intentions – we were leaving – and I was concerned not to leak anything to the Press before a public announcement. Surprisingly they had not picked up on our plans, despite the activity in the Residence. I am sure the Foreign Office was worried that I was sailing close to the wind, as by then I was appearing internationally on every news channel, every day, as well as all over the newspapers. From their point of view it was preferable for reasons of security that the official spokesman in London was the only mouthpiece in a crisis.

SUNDAY 21 APRIL

The next day the news broke that by Sunday 28 April embassies in both London and Tripoli would close. The thought of packing up 25 households, including three absentees, within a week, appalled us. The Cooling family had just begun unpacking after their year-long traipse round Tripoli. "Well, at least they've got some boxes," someone said.

The first thing was for Paul to find some packers. There were only two companies in Tripoli, but one agreed to take the job on. They were to start at the Residence on Monday morning. Little did we know that the Libyans would restrict our movements again. Ian phoned early that evening from the Office.

"Small problem – can't get out. Can I speak to Oliver, please?" He did not seem unduly worried.

"Who's in the Office?" I heard Oliver ask. "Good. At least one Administration Officer is free. Paul can run round and Red can do the inside work. But awful for you stuck inside again ..."

Morale was always good. Everyone supported everyone else physically and psychologically. But the fact remained that 10 people were again locked in the Office and would stay there for another four nights.

Oliver pointed out to me the unfairness of the situation based supposedly on a reciprocal arrangement.

"If the truth were known, the Libyans have three official establishments in different parts of London and only one of them is ringed by police. Their consular and commercial departments are operating as freely as ever. Because we only have one building, we are hamstrung."

I was glad when I got an opportunity to leak this to BBC Radio 4's *World at One*.

"How do you mean 'locked up', Mrs Miles?" Robin Day's voice, firm and direct, also had a sardonic edge.

"Literally. Ten staff have been stuck in the Office ever since the announcement of the break in diplomatic relations was made."

Over the next few days Oliver managed to negotiate a head-for-head swap amongst the staff so that Ian could shore up Barbara who was beginning to flag at home with two kids. Paul took his place so that he could help Red with administrative matters. During this time the only person whose freedom was guaranteed was Oliver and he regarded his police escort as protective rather than punitive.

Monday 22 April

On Monday morning we mustered what boxes and trunks we had. They were soon filled and we remarked on the non-appearance of the promised packing company. Valuable time was slipping by and I had to sell as much of our three years' worth of stock as I could. It had taken me three months and half a year's salary to acquire it before leaving England, physically lugging much of it between shops and home. I had tried to anticipate every future requirement, including substantial items like two 20 cu ft freezers and an African-specification seven-seater Peugeot.

Consumer goods (along with everything else) were in such short supply in Libya that firms as well as individuals were prepared to buy up complete households – everything from radio batteries to frozen raspberries, no questions asked. I thus managed to sell most of our household goods in one fell swoop.

The problem was physically shifting them. Nearly everything was kept in upstairs bedroom cupboards as we had so little kitchen storage space. A few weeks earlier, Sarah and I had lugged it all up, and now it looked as if we had to carry it all down again.

In the middle of packing, Daniela and Mia, two wives from the Italian Embassy dropped in to help. They looked enviably *soigné* in contrast to me, but it was lovely to see them. The British government had put feelers out to the Italian government to become our protecting power, so they said it was logical for them to come, but it was no less kind.

"We've been trying to make contact all along. We were turned away that fateful Wednesday morning. Give us a list of things you want to sell …" They were brisk and efficient. "We'll be back tomorrow morning to go through the house with you. You'd better remove the valuables as the Libyans are bound to vandalise the place, as they did with the American Ambassador's Residence."

This was a genuine risk and I had to think of a way of protecting government property. To get our personal stuff shipped out was going to be a superhuman task but to add all the Residence furniture seemed almost foolhardy.

The Italians were happy to act as postmen: this was a relief. I did not feel like driving all over Tripoli, even if I was allowed – it was never made clear. I felt apprehensive about leaving the children at home, just in case I was held and we were separated. So, solidarity was the name of the game. Gratefully, I loaded my Italian friends into their car with a list of errands and waved them off.

I stopped them just as they were starting to move. "Nora phoned me this morning and told me the sad news about the wedding dress being stolen from Monika's car in Rome." Monika, the Italian Ambassador's wife, had returned home to arrange her daughter's wedding.

"Yes, terrible news. She's having it remade – the wedding's next Friday and Sacha is terribly worried he won't be there to give his only daughter away." Sacha was the Italian Ambassador.

"It's awful how often there's a clash of interests between official duty and personal life. It's something that really bugs our service."

They nodded sympathetically. We diplomatic wives feel the Office usually wins in such circumstances and there is no redress. I was surprised how guilty I felt about the possibility of Sacha missing his daughter's wedding because he had got caught up in a British political row.

Frank Marshall was resorting to devious means. Prospective purchasers of provisions were being deterred from entering his house by the Revolutionary Committee guards. So he worked out a plan.

"Can the kids come and play at the Residence?" he asked.

"Sure. See you later this morning."

Before he arrived I received a phone call from his wife, Clare. "Tell Frank 'mission accomplished'."

I thought perhaps she had had their dog put down and didn't want the children to witness the event.

When I told Frank, he laughed. "The dog's going to a good home, don't worry. No, we've been selling some stuff and I thought if I lured the guards away, because I knew they would follow me here, Clare could get on with the business."

I realised that we too would probably have to resort to cloak-and-dagger behaviour. Not only did our guards deny access to some callers, but there was always a risk that they would be searched on departure. Once again I found I could get a dialling tone only intermittently. It was becoming quite clear that the Libyans were intent on being as obstructive as possible.

TUESDAY 23 APRIL

Paul had tipped off jolly, plump Andree in the Belgian Embassy that alcohol would be available at the Residence. "I'll come as soon as I can arrange transport," she told me.

Andree had been in charge of American interests since the US had broken off diplomatic relations some years earlier. She had been left with the dubious privilege of owning the departed Ambassador's Cadillac which, after a recent highway contretemps, only worked in reverse gear. I never actually saw her backing up the street to a diplomatic function, but I gather that out of desperation she had occasionally done so. She did not arrive that morning. The first visitors were the Italian wives. "We've sold one of your freezers," they reported. "To our Ambassador!"

Juma was the Embassy 'fixer'. All over the world one finds these odd individuals who know their way round the local system. They are invaluable and few Embassies would manage without someone who can duck and dive through the local bureaucracy. Somehow Juma found boxes and sticky tape, and got through the police cordon by the gate. It was better not to ask how. We started emptying the cupboards.

Then BBC TV appeared. "Can we have a picture of you packing?"

"I've more or less done it."

"Well, never mind, just empty out a caseload and do it again. And could you do it in another room? The light's not very good in here."

I gave them a killer look.

"Oh, come on, it's what the public likes."

"I'm jolly well going to join Equity," I grumbled. "Anyway, why don't you film the contents of this cupboard?" I swung open a door to reveal £150 worth of loo rolls. Kate Adie burst out laughing.

"Come on, boys. We have to get a shot of this."

Anne Raynouard, a French friend with gamine haircut and slight, boyish figure, appeared.

"I've come to 'elp. Straight from ze Sahara," she announced.

I did not demur. The phone was ringing, the kids fighting, the dog barking, the servants shouting, doors slamming. I directed her to the loo-roll cupboard and fled.

Next at the door were the Australian Potts family, looking for food.

"Upstairs," I shouted and ran to answer the door bell again.

"Ah, Andree."

"Mr Mecklenbourg wants the drink, not me." (He was the Belgian Ambassador).

I had no idea what price to charge a diplomatic colleague.

The phone rang and it was Paul.

"Any packers arrived?"

"No, but chaos. Lucky you rang, I can't find the price list for the 'you know what' and Andree is here."

"Oh, the unmentionables. Just say £2 per unit if you get my meaning."

I didn't have the time or inclination to argue.

Frank Marshall was listening. I seemed to have netted an extra four children.

"You've got to charge more for the good wine."

The Madge family materialised; three more kids. "Join the party ..."

Roger Madge said very quietly, almost conspiratorially, "Have you any use for an old tin trunk?"

"Absolutely! None of us has nearly enough packing materials. We've got to pack up the Wright's flat upstairs and they're in Rome. I just don't know how we are going to do it. Where is it?"

"I haven't actually got it here …"

"Well, get it here …"

"We're off now," announced Keith Potts. "Be back for more. I'm not too sure about the beer kits."

"I thought that would just do the trick for some of your desert chaps."

"Yeah. But I've got to get out of your front gate." He gestured helplessly.

"Let Annie take them. She's got diplomatic number plates."

Annie's car was so weighed down with baked beans and Dettol that it broke down while being unloaded. Mysteriously, the beer kits emerged at the Italian Embassy, under Daniela's care. She was apologetic.

"I don't care where anything goes so long as it just goes and it does someone some good."

"It's our National Day party soon," said Daniela, "so Monika wants us to take anything suitable. I presume your Queen's Birthday Party is off?"

"Well it was, but ever since Dr Treiki started telling Oliver how much he's looking forward to coming we've had to keep our options open. But honestly the last thing I want to do is put on my glad rags and sip cocktails tomorrow night."

When Oliver came in for lunch I tackled him.

"It's all very well your idea about going down with all flags waving," I said. "But I need to know if this party is on or off. I can just see what's going to happen. Half the staff are locked in the Embassy, you'll say you're caught up with something pressing and I'll be left with the Cuban Ambassador, making chit-chat and pretending everything is normal. No thanks."

"We're a step ahead of you. It's cancelled."

"Has every single guest been notified?" Since the switchboard was constantly jammed, I doubted it and had visions of British community ladies in flowery hats fighting their way past Revolutionary guards, only to find me and the kids lying on the floor playing tiddlywinks.

Paul rang. "I'll be with you at seven." He told me to report his non-arrival if he failed to meet the deadline. By 7.02 pm I was beginning to fret but a minute later he breezed in carrying what looked like a parcel of laundry. It was an enormous bouquet of red roses and pink carnations.

"Real flowers!" I gasped. In the Middle East fresh flowers assume great glamour because of their scarcity and inflated prices. Paul was off hand.

"You remember when the Chief Medical Officer stayed last month?"

I did, it had been a welcome bonus.

"Well, he gave me the money to buy these for you and I've just found it in the back of a drawer."

"Paul, this is the perfect moment. I appreciate them more now than I would have a month ago. Thank you so much."

I cannot imagine where Paul found them. I had never seen flowers on sale in Tripoli and these were so beautifully fresh that they were still looking good the day we left Libya; the only frill in a desolate landscape.

Oliver was grumbling good-naturedly when he came home. "Nobody knew where Paul had got to. The fact that he had gone to buy flowers for you makes me less cross."

"He said he only did it to see if he could shake off his tail."

"Anyway, what about this packing?" Oliver said. "I'm jolly well going to pinch that signed photo of the Queen."

I was flabbergasted by this uncharacteristic move by my husband, who is scrupulous about probity. But I knew he would declare the transgression when he got back to London.

48 Hours to Evacuate

WEDNESDAY 24 APRIL

Everyone suddenly realised how short time was getting, and there was a noticeable move by the Press to put their shoulder to the wheel to help me. They could see that Oliver was too busy, and I felt as if I was keeping numerous plates spinning simultaneously. The three big North American TV consortia were pressed into unbolting the four largest pictures from the walls, including the portraits of George V and Queen Mary under the direction of Kate Adie and Abdullah. Keith, a photographer, together with Mia from the Italian Embassy and our 12-year-old son Joe, were recruited to make an inventory of everything that was to be left behind in the house.

This sudden injection of muscle power cleared the backlog and freed up the Residence staff to pack the two upstairs flats. One belonged to the absent Wrights, and the other to Muriel, Oliver's secretary, who having been freed from the Office was ordered back in again to do the typing. Sarah the cook took on the job of selling stuff. Daniela and Mia reappeared to consider the removal of valuable government property. The Danish Ambassador and his wife Hannah, although new to Tripoli, were very solicitous. They impressed on me that they had storage space in their back bedroom where they would willingly house any good pieces. All our diplomatic colleagues were certain that the Libyans would wreck the house as soon as we left, so I gratefully accepted their offer.

My next problem was to find a lorry to shift the stuff. I knew none of our staff had time to load and drive the British Embassy truck. The Italians said they had only a tiny pick-up and whatever vehicle the Danes had was on loan to their farming project somewhere south of Tripoli. Daniela and Mia were unfazed. They enlisted the help of their Administration Officer, a warm-hearted gentleman who kissed and cuddled anyone within reach and positively bear-hugged the children, much to their horror.

"Leave it to Bruno!" he shouted. "Let Bruno do it!"

It was most reassuring to have a shoulder to lean on. And Bruno did do it: he found a lorry and a crane for the heavy jobs and enlisted a team of helpers to choose, lift and carry items. Hannah was scurrying back and forth all day in her tiny car laden with priceless Chinese vases, antique carriage clocks and even the red leather Visitor's Book that lay in the Residence entrance hall.

With the aid of the lorry we were able to remove some of the large items: a Chinese lacquer cabinet, a hand-painted 18th-century grandfather clock that Oliver had painstakingly repaired during the first days of our posting, any paintings which could be easily moved, some red damask sofas and the William and Mary hall chairs. But the larger items remained a problem.

Daniela was firmly of the opinion that the grand piano was too heavy to move. Bruno disagreed. "If we leave it here, the Libyans will think it's booby trapped; they won't even dare raise the lid before they blow it up. Bruno will move it."

He did, too. By luck the Indian Ambassador, who had come to say goodbye to us, incautiously enquired about the piano's destiny. I jumped:

"You're a bachelor living in a big house, aren't you? Please, take the piano."

"My pleasure." He swallowed uneasily. Too late. However, he dug his heels in at my suggestion that he might also like to house the life-size oil paintings of George V and Queen Mary, which took up the whole of one wall.

"That would be a political act, he declared. The Raj ..." He waved his hand vaguely. I took the hint.

Ian had parked his Volvo in our drive before his incarceration. I found him unlocking it late in the afternoon, looking extremely pale and haggard.

"Congratulations on your release."

"It's been harder for Barbara. She's done terribly well on the packing. She's been all alone and under great strain."

"I wonder whether on your way home you could go via the Andersons? I've just had a call from George to say they are desperate for packing materials. Nobody can get in to him. Would you take these boxes and tape and throw them over his garden wall?"

The Libyan packers had eventually sent a lorry with the cardboard boxes we had ordered. They left it at the Residence and we were cheerfully helping ourselves rather than waiting for them to return. Ian dutifully loaded his car with the few boxes that remained in the unattended lorry.

"They're not going to be pleased when they come back and find their supplies gone," I remarked.

"Honestly Julia, I couldn't care less. We've got to be able to pack up in time

Sue Pigott sounded more cock-a-hoop than ever at that evening's daily phone-in. "I knew I had the makings of a burglar," she declared. "I've broken into the Burtons' house, taken the back off a desk, rescued their jewels and the cats, and I've been cutting pictures out of their frames with a razor blade. It's difficult to know what else to take. Half the stuff belongs to the Libyan landlord, on the other hand I have the strong impression that all the Burtons' worldly goods are in this house."

I was full of admiration. I applaud people who take a grip of life and get on with things. "What about your own packing?"

"Oh, fine. Carsten and I got it done. It was lucky he wasn't one of the people locked in the Office. I felt so sorry for Barbara, on her own."

"George (the Consul), "is *incommunicado* too – he can't get out of his house at all. His nanny and daughter have been trying to get to England as they are both due to take their A levels, but every day they are turned back at the airport."

This obstructiveness had incensed Oliver as it was unnecessarily spiteful and could well have jeopardised the girls' careers. He had tackled Prime Minister Treiki without success. Even Jeff Asmah, the Ghanaian Ambassador, had tried escorting them to the airport with full diplomatic panoply, but to no effect.

It was a constant complaint of ours that we were forced to live in a country where the people were too scared to communicate with us. One of our oldest friends, recently retired from the diplomatic service, confided before we left for Libya that he looked back over his career with regret. We were amazed. "Regret? Why?" He had seemed so successful, so in tune with places where he had served.

"Because as a diplomat, you are always an outsider."

I am afraid it is true. Three years in a post is not long enough to dig sufficiently deep to get to know a society, let alone one culturally and linguistically alien to one's own. However well-disposed both sides are, the very knowledge of impermanence casts a blight on a deep relationship. And yet, how many of us really regret moving on?

The British ex-pat community was shocked at the imminent closure of the Embassy. It was not just that the Office offered consular help and commercial support, but the staff acted as the focal point of social life. We had houses large enough in which to entertain, and a certain amount of alcohol, and it was one of the duties of our posting – indeed most of us had entertainment allowances to enable us to do so. We had all been in other posts, some exceedingly trying, and knew how important it was to keep morale high and the flag flying. Somewhere I found an anonymous quote which says: "Diplomacy is more often concerned with the difficult, depressed and deranged than the dashing, dapper, dandified image suggests."

We counted an average of 80 people in the Residence every week: not many compared to a large post with political clout, but significant enough with the resources available. Usually, there is more hospitality and mutual self-help in a difficult post. If an entire Embassy disappears, it creates an enormous vacuum in the community left behind. A delegation came to see me at lunchtime, led by the formidable Margot who ran the library and had been a stalwart of the community since the days of King Idris. She had not left Libya for 27 years.

"Would you mind telling me what all this nonsense is about?" she began, banging her walking stick on the floor for emphasis. "It's a great mistake and quite unnecessary. And what is to happen to the library, may I ask?"

I had been helping over the past few weeks to catalogue a load of shiny new books, down in the bowels of the Residence where the library was housed. To Margot's horror I had insisted on expanding the children's section and had ordered £300 worth of paperbacks, most of which were still wrapped up, and all unread. I supposed that if the Libyans wanted to be really difficult they could burn the books on the grounds that they were obscene. I just hoped they would not.

"I have an offer from the French Cultural Institute. If they can gain access after we're gone, they'll get the books out."

Margot snorted. I did not tell her that the French counsellor, together with the Greek *Chargé d'Affaires*, had already twice been refused entry by the police. Even Jeff Asmah had faced difficulties getting to see Oliver, while the Italians had been locked inside our Embassy for three hours the previous day. Later we were told that the Libyans believed that they were mirroring the treatment that their People's Bureau was receiving from the British police and government.

The Vienna Convention was frequently invoked by the British during this time. The convention guaranteed some basic freedom and protection for diplomats in the host country, but to get the wilder men of the Revolutionary Committees to accept the printed word was difficult. It seemed they preferred a half-baked attempt at tit-for-tat reciprocity rather than the generally accepted diplomatic notion that activities should be conducted on the basis of 'mutual advantage'. Since police guards had been put on Libyan houses in London, they did the same to us. But were the tactics of the Libyan police complementary to those of the Met? I wondered how many Libyan households in London were being prevented from packing up.

Many individuals Oliver dealt with in the Foreign Liaison Bureau were sophisticated, decent and intelligent. But their agreements would be overruled by the wilder People's Committee members and subsequently reneged on. Another problem, he believed, was that the police received their instructions too late. The bureaucratic structure was not efficient. Sometimes after a teleconference with the FCO he needed to relay some well-argued principle to Dr Treiki, but spent ages on time-wasting negotiations to get the Embassy front door opened (quite literally), even when the principle had been established between him and Dr Treiki. No wonder Oliver was getting short-tempered.

THURSDAY 25 APRIL

It occurred to me that a daily pattern was emerging. At dawn the phone would ring from another part of the world. Our early breakfast would end in disarray because of an unexpected arrival. The morning would be spent thinking on my feet, talking to the Press, organising staff, feeding the rabbit or child visitors, answering the phone and concealing things which were in current use to prevent them from being packed. I would answer the door, divine visitors' motives, ease them out if they weren't there to help, make lists, sell things and so on. Lunch would be skipped because it was too embarrassing to eat in front of a dozen hungry Pressmen. Getting to the loo was a treat as there was barely time between phone calls.

The afternoon was a continuation of the morning, except that Oliver would appear and disappear like the

Cheshire Cat. One moment I would see him escorting the Kuwaiti Ambassador into the garden, the next he'd melted away towards the Foreign Liaison Bureau. Yet every visitor cross-questioned me: "When will he back?" "Wish I knew." "Does that indicate some development?" "You'll have to ask him." And so on. The telephone version – usually from some American ladies' magazine – went like this: "When did he last come home?"... "How did he seem?"... "If you look deep into his eyes, what do you see?" Honestly!

There would be a lull around 'cocktail hour', presumably because that is when the Press filed their stories. In most other countries they would be propping up a bar. During the day, if they weren't at the Residence they would scour Tripoli for new angles, so they would attend Dr Treiki's press conference or visit the People's Palace to watch Gaddafi acknowledge his subjects' fealty (in reality a dozen paid sycophants who had to play-act their devotion).

After a slow and sticky start, the media lost their coyness. Terry Lloyd of ITN even got arrested and thrown into prison for doing what he was good at: investigating. The battered bus had finally been produced by the Information Department, but far from obeying Libyan orders, the Press Corps was pretty well directing the bus driver wherever they wanted to go.

Sometimes they were escorted by the Libyans to witness interesting events. On one occasion they were taken to Green Square to watch a demonstration. They were just setting up their cameras when Mohamed said, "Get back on the bus. Sorry, wrong demonstration." There was no evidence of any anti-British feeling and no popular protests round the Embassy, only the restrictions they had placed on our freedom of movement.

Anne Raynouard returned to say goodbye. She had news: "I 'eard from ze French teachers in Benghazi zat zere was some 'angings earlier zis week. I am sure it is true."

We had already heard this, from expatriate friends who lived on the Tripoli University campus. On the anniversary of the Jamahiriya, Gaddafi had visited the university for celebrations.

Not only were there none, but someone had defaced his portrait. Just as in the previous year, he ordered the execution of a couple of students. A relative of one of the victims retaliated, firing a machine gun on the crowd who were being forced to watch the hangings as a deterrent. He killed and injured several people.

None of this was publicly admitted by the Libyans, nor had it reached the Western press. When David Willey, the BBC Rome correspondent, came to interview me I decided to tell him. I suggested that there might have been some link between these events and the fatal anti-Gaddafi demonstration in London. He took this seriously enough to put it in a front-page article in *The Observer*.

The Spanish Ambassador and his wife (clad in eye-watering purple couture) paid a visit. It might seem incongruous to have held an impromptu tea party at this juncture, but that was the scene: immaculate guests and a fidgety hostess covered in dust.

"Is there anything we can do?" they enquired kindly. They turned out to be my saviours since most of the Embassy furniture ended up crammed into their cellar for much longer than they had bargained for. The Foreign Office failed to relieve them of the burden, as promised, and their piteous cries followed me into our next posting a year later, much to my dismay.

The diplomatic staff were shredding and burning the Embassy archives, the girls working barefoot as their feet ached from all the standing. At the end of the day one found that her left shoe had disappeared. "It's been shredded, of course!" Muriel, Oliver's secretary, flushed with gin and tiredness, regaled us with tales of the Office as we grilled the last piece of fillet steak (hoarded for some future diplomatic function) on the barbecue by the swimming pool. This was the only means of cooking as the gas stove borrowed from Helen, the immensely efficient and helpful British Caledonian ground hostess, had been spirited away the previous day.

That evening Oliver came home to confirm that most of the women and children would be leaving the following day, Friday

26 April. There was a huge sigh of relief. Since the children had had no toys and no outlet for their keyed-up energy for a week, hanging around any longer was a dreadful thought. Three months earlier I had booked my two older sons on to the very same scheduled flight to return to boarding school in England. Somehow that date had became a fixed departure time in everyone's minds. The Press had got wind of it and given it significance; if the date had slipped there would have been conjecture and speculation as to the reason. Ascribing meaning to something trivial so that it has an effect on more important matters is a dangerous aspect of Press attention.

After supper I washed my hair and went downstairs with a towel round my head. The Press was there in force: television cameras ready to devour anything that hove into view. They burst out laughing at my appearance.

"Look, you go and take care of yourself for once," said Keith Miller from one of the big American networks. "Your boys will entertain us."

The Press's long wait for Oliver was finally rewarded but not before they had drained our liquor store dry, leaving us to destroy the evidence. We all felt blue; it was like the end of a party. We exchanged addresses.

"Let's get together over a bowl of pasta in Rome," Keith said. "And don't forget that video of all of your TV appearances."

Maria Ioannides gave us a standing invitation to Paris, and Kate Adie suggested we have a day at the BBC, perhaps at half-term, with the boys. "But," everyone chorused as they trooped out, "we'll see you at the airport tomorrow."

FRIDAY 26 APRIL

D-Day.

The Australian Broadcasting Corporation gave us our wake-up call. Oliver's voiced creaked with tiredness; I hoped they weren't looking for a live interview. Then I heard him say, "The worst thing is the cancellation of the cricket match between you and us. It was meant to be played tomorrow."

I sat up in bed. "What on earth are you talking about?"

"They wanted to know what effect the rumpus would have on the British community and I am trying to think of a new answer."

"And what did he say?"

"Surely, Mr Miles, the situation is more serious than that."

Well, was it? Throughout all my interviews I had striven to present a balanced account. Letting the Press sensationalise events could endanger the fragile negotiations intended to get us home safely. I had on several occasions asked them to keep their coverage low key; I had also been at pains to stress the normality and lack of panic in Tripoli. But this, of course, does not sell newspapers.

None of us felt any real physical threat and most of the Libyans we encountered were as friendly as ever. Our strong impression was that if the local population had any interest at all in what was happening, they were not necessarily on Gaddafi's side. A Libyan woman sweeping the pavement in her dressing gown had given Fiona Davies the 'thumbs up' the day after the 'siege' began.

It was difficult to gauge what the Libyans had been told. One of the cameramen said that the Libyans had booked him to cover the St James's Square demonstration and he had recorded the dreadful moment of WPC Fletcher's murder. His film had been shown uncut every night on Libyan TV more as a warning than as public information. The only other public information came from JANA, the Libyan News Agency. But their highly coloured account of any event carried little conviction. We imagined that any motivated and interested Libyan would tune into the BBC World Service or watch Italian TV for a fuller account: a mid-evening sight in Tripoli was the simultaneous swivelling of satellite dishes towards Europe as residents tuned in to watch the evening news.

"Can anyone tell me what the hell is happening?" Carsten was rattled. "Frank is standing in his best bib and tucker obviously thinking he's about to leave. Who's leaving? Is anyone?"

It's awful when Embassy communication fails but I suppose it had been under strain. "All wives, children and nannies are to rendezvous here at 10.30am."

By 10.30 the back of the Residence resembled a large-scale Sunday School picnic. Kids were dashing around, some in tears, mothers anxiously chain smoking, a baby gazing up at a lemon tree from its cot, husbands humping bags and boxes and trying to reverse their cars in too tight a space. The scheduled flight left at 1.30pm so we hoped to be on our way by 11.30. At noon, news came that the incoming flight had been delayed because some CBS newsman refused to disembark.

John Blackstone from CBS, was suitably contrite. "Can I make amends?" he offered. "Lunch for everyone at the Hotel Kabir?"

It was generous of John and I felt guilty that, on instruction, I had made the news public. But in the end it seemed easier for me to lay on a picnic for all present, Press Corps included. We could use up food that would otherwise have been wasted. There were cases of Pepsi and fizzy orange from the upstairs flats and I had somehow overlooked six pounds of cheese and two-dozen eggs. Someone had found some bread and there were Mars bars. No fruit, as oranges had gone out of season, but there was tea and coffee.

I donned a tea towel apron to prepare the meagre feast and immediately the kitchen was full of wives, helping. We could not but remark on the absence of those paid to help, as we could see them chain smoking like mad on the lower garden wall. Evidently they felt their contract was at an end. Oh well, we sighed, we were probably as irresponsible when we were young.

At 1pm we finally moved off in convoy, led by the dapper Signor Kardilli, sporting a memorable designer silk tie. He had been recalled from the Italian Embassy in the Netherlands to organise our withdrawal. An Arabist who had served in Tripoli previously, he was totally on top of the job. His arrival had allowed Sacha, the Italian Ambassador, to get to his daughter's wedding in Rome the next day – a 36-hour dash. I was relieved to hear it.

It took ages to reach the airport. Finally we were escorted upstairs to a small separate lounge which was jam-packed with chairs and a couple of plastic fir trees in polystyrene snow which kept the kids occupied for a while. The scheduled flight had already departed, but there was another aircraft standing by for our departure. A number of European colleagues had come to see us off, as had the Press Corps, whom I had already primed.

"It's wonderful having you around. You've been a great support. Please see that we get on that plane – don't leave until we do. And if anything happens – record it as fully as possible."

The overcrowded room grew hotter and hotter. By 4pm we were quite demoralised. Fiona was gallantly doing her playschool act in the marble floored lounge: "You put your right leg in ..."

Helen, the British Caledonian ground hostess and a legend amongst the British community, was as unruffled as ever, discreetly pointing Oliver in the direction of useful Libyans. The airport director, Colonel Mansour, strolled coolly through our midst in a white suit and high-heeled boots, carrying a walkie-talkie.

"Did you know he carries a white radio when wearing his white outfit and a black radio with his black outfit?" Oliver said.

I suppose it was the stress and apprehension of waiting, but this arrogant character incensed me. I followed Oliver into the police room.

"You really are a load of shits," I said, noting their lack of concern. Nobody so much as flicked an eyelid. I cornered the German Ambassador.

"I've just told them what I think of them."

"Vere is your famous British phlegm now?" He stared meaningfully at me. I gave him a look but took the point.

"Zese men are bullies. Zey enjoy it more ven you get angry. Be careful for your husband's sake. Remember ve do not yet know ven he vill leave."

But Oliver was also getting angry at our treatment. Much later we learned that the Libyans were not going to allow us to leave until the female dependants of the People's Bureau staff had taken off from Heathrow. The British police were keeping the men behind for extra security.

"I'm not pulling any punches," Oliver said to me.

"I hope the pressure is not getting to you. I don't want you to drop down dead."

He grinned. "Actually I'm quite enjoying it. I don't often get the chance to swear in Arabic."

Helen had arranged for sandwiches and sticky drinks, and we fell on them eagerly. "I bet this bit of reciprocity is not reciprocal," I remarked. "London airport sandwiches aren't half as well filled."

Oliver burst out of the police room.

"You'll never guess what! The sandwich man actually had the gall to ask for payment for the sandwiches!"

"And what did you do?"

"I complained to the police. They said if that were so, it must be because he is Tunisian."

At 5pm there were two minor breakthroughs: the luggage could be loaded and Joe discovered a drinking fountain.

The Libyans refused to load the luggage on board, so again the Press stepped in to help our husbands do it. I noticed that some members of the Diplomatic Corps had disappeared, but they had been resolute in their support and that counted for a lot. After their gallantry in loading the plane, most of the Press were ignominiously locked out on the terrace in the dark. They reappeared blue with cold, and Mohamed ordered them to board the bus. They refused.

"I bet they'll make us wait till the Libyan plane from London lands," I said nervously.

"I don't think so." But Oliver was grim.

"It's getting so late I'd better phone my mother to tell her not to expect us tonight."

The police would not let us use their phones and told us all the other phones were cut off. They directed me to the post office where a youth sulkily dialled the number. I spoke to my mother from a separate booth.

"I'm still in Tripoli," I kept yelling. She half got my message.

"That will be two and a half dinars," said the youth.

"Charge it to Colonel Mansour's account," said Oliver without hesitation.

"Who's he?"

"The man over there in the white suit."

I have never seen anyone jump up and down with rage before.

The German, Belgian and Dutch Ambassadors were still stoically waiting. "They really are getting their pound of flesh," I said to them. "It's terribly good of you to stay."

"It's the least we can do." The unkind thought flashed through my mind that they wanted to see the final drama – perhaps we would all be blown up or machine-gunned. Anything could happen. But then I thought how fortunate we were to have such solid support: it might make all the difference if there was a real crisis.

And then at last! A move! What intense relief. But what fear and sadness: the men were staying behind.

"Well guys, this is it," announced an American pressman. "Was it Mark Twain who said that everyone can expect 10 minutes of fame in their life? I guess you've just had yours." Before anyone could tell him it was Andy Warhol (who specified 15 minutes), there was a general effort to move.

"Not quite she hasn't," said Keith the cameraman. "There's going to be a hell of a reception at Gatwick." He handed me a package. "Here, can you take these films and hand them over at the airport?"

"What about her courier fee?" someone joked.

"Don't forget to get in touch and we'll let you have some photos as a reward."

"I'd rather have fifty quid."

Helen was firm. "I've made hotel reservations for you all. Now if you have your boarding cards, please get on the plane."

I went into the waiting room where most of the wives were gathered. "Does anyone feel like singing something? What words do we know?"

It felt the right thing to do at the time but it turned out to be a rather feeble rendition of *Rule Britannia* and the National Anthem. Later on, it earned me quite a lot of scorn.

HOMEWARD BOUND
AND HOMELESS

Everyone came out onto the tarmac. I kissed as many staff and Press as I could manage in the confusion. They were a super bunch. Kate Adie shouted, "I'll call you to come and look round the BBC."

"Keep going, old boy." I hugged Oliver and climbed the steps. At the top I turned and waved. "I'll see you Sunday." No sooner had the words escaped than I kicked myself – maybe I had compromised their chances of leaving. The aircraft was mostly empty. We were scattered about in seemingly haphazard fashion, but Helen had emphasised how important this weight distribution was. It reinforced the unsettling feeling of our not really knowing what was going on. I was on the wrong side to see out of the window as we took off and just glimpsed Oliver's olive-green suit. I saw Helen dissolve into tears and it dawned on me what a vacuum our departure had left.

"Now," said Sue Pigott, "for the champagne."

"I don't think there's anything to celebrate till the men leave," replied Barbara, her eyes glistening.

"Come on, Barbara, surely you're glad that we're going home?"

There were three half-bottles of champagne on the plane, so we each got a mouthful. The Libyans had not allowed any newspapers on board. This disappointed me as I had not seen a paper for three weeks, so I had to settle for a copy of an old *Daily Telegraph* that someone had found at the airport. Inside was an article about Hattie, our dog and Honeybun, the rabbit, entitled 'All About the Animals'.

Little did I know what was in store. We had left Hattie in the care of the night watchman who had just lost his son, and seemed glad of the company. We left Honeybun hopping about the large grassy garden, confident that she would sustain herself until rescued by Said the farmer, or someone. I did not foresee the Press as their abductors.

"We are crossing into Tunisia," announced the Captain.

"Thank God," said Sue, unloading one of the kids into the aisle. "At least we're out of range of Libyan MiGS."

It was a treat having an airliner to ourselves. Each time Catherine Marshall, aged eight and dressed as a British Caledonian stewardess, passed without spilling Coca Cola into my lap, I praised God.

"For goodness sake, Catherine, be careful. I've got to go on television at the airport – OK?"

Although I had been tipped off that there would be a large Press reception at Gatwick, nobody had warned me that we would also be met by the Minister of State, Richard Luce, and a number of senior Foreign Office officials. When we landed, the stewardess came to say that I should get off the plane first. Joe got out the Union Jack he'd found in the Residence's larder and ordered Tom to wave it. Lucy, who had finally dropped off to sleep as we began our descent, was furious to be woken up, and roared.

Stepping out of the plane onto the steps with two children in my arms, I was blinded by illuminations. It was now 11.30pm in the UK and early morning in Tripoli. We had been up for nearly 24 hours. There was an orderly line of Press to my right and at the bottom of the steps the Ministerial Daimler and a group of people, some of whom I knew.

Sir John Leahy, Oliver's recent boss, said to me, "Now please introduce the staff to the Minister as they emerge."

The next person coming down the steps was the Andersons' nanny.

"This is Joy, the nanny," I said lamely.

"Let's give it up," he replied testily.

The Press were shouting: "Mrs Miles, Mrs Miles, look this way."

Then I was shoved unceremoniously into the Daimler with my four kids. It all happened so suddenly the children forgot to argue over who should get the fold-down seats. I found myself sitting on Mr Luce's right thigh but he did not seem to notice, and within seconds we were deposited at the VIP suite, where Foreign Office Welfare Department staff were out in force. I tried to thank Jim, the Chief Medical Officer, for the flowers that Paul had bought on his behalf. He brushed it aside. No one was listening to anyone else. There seemed to be dozens of policemen.

Sir John Leahy asked conspiratorially: "Did Oliver send any message to me?"

I searched my fuzzy memory.

"Not that I know of. They are all convinced that they won't be out till Sunday. Their morale is good." What could have been a dramatic, tension-filled sequence in a good thriller was, in real life, a bit pedestrian.

Richard Luce said, "Choose two wives to come into the press conference with you."

"I'm going to be sick," Hugh, aged six, announced.

"Find a corner darling ..."

I wondered why none of the Foreign Office ladies who were standing around looking pleasant did anything to help. They seemed strangely dressed up for the occasion: some were wearing cocktail dresses. And rows of bottles were laid out, suggesting a reception rather than a rescue unit. Most of us wanted aspirin and Tampax, not gin and tonic.

"Barbara and Sue, come into the lions' den."

"Emma's just thrown up all down my front," said Sue.

"Zip up your windcheater and no one will know except it does smell a bit strong."

I kept wishing I could remember whether Richard Luce had been knighted as it was impossible to attract his attention. Then I hit on the old trick.

"Ah, Minister ..."

"Remember not to say anything that will compromise the men's return," he instructed me tersely.

Man at my foot: "Psst, have you got Keith's negatives?" I passed over a small package, trying not to look surreptitious. "Rest in the baggage – see you later," I hissed back, hoping nobody overheard. The questions were straight and friendly: they were all directed at me but I tried to involve Barbara and Sue as much as possible. I was almost asphyxiated by the stench of Emma's sick, which kept wafting over me.

"How's Mr Miles?" asked one. I didn't want to admit publicly that he was enjoying himself. Diplomats like crises: that is what they join for.

We reached the subject of reciprocity but before I could open my mouth, Mr Luce intervened – evidently the subject was political quicksand. We got through it and were bundled out, back to the cocktail-dress brigade.

One said, "You asked for an advance of £200 on your husband's salary. Sign here, please." It was true, I had. Aware that I had no sterling I had phoned Barclays Bank that morning (I could hardly believe it was still the same day) to get some help. The conversation had been quite futile – I spoke to some junior who said she did not think they covered Libya – until a senior man grabbed the phone and assured me I could have money on demand. But to be sure I had some cash, I took up the Office's invitation to borrow some.

"And here's your mail."

A diplomatic bag containing mail had been stopped from leaving London on the day WPC Fletcher had been killed, so there was quite a pile of stuff. It was almost uplifting to see the Barclaycard envelope and dear old Hart District Council's stationery. There was a wider world outside, and soon we would be back in it. But I wished this well-meaning woman had thought to put the money and mail into a plastic bag; I had at least one child in my arms and it was spilling everywhere.

"We're fed up with waiting," Joe wailed. In Libyan time it must have been nearly dawn.

"I really am going to be sick this time …"

For the children's sake we had to move, and so under the watchful eye of the police, we and a few others whose relatives had not come to collect them were dispatched to the Hilton Hotel. Later I was informed that Martin, my brother-in-law, had offered to meet us but had been told that the Office would look after us. Over the next decade, I regularly met friends who told me that their offers of transport and accommodation had been refused on my behalf – and without my knowledge – by the Foreign Office welfare machine.

"It's very posh, this hotel," said Catherine Marshall airily. "We always stay here." Diplomatic children do acquire a certain *savoir faire*. Perhaps it serves to insulate them from the knocks and losses they experience due to their parents' profession. The hotel was not exactly posh but it certainly was efficient.

"Can I help you in anyway?" enquired a woman in Caledonian Airlines uniform. At last some down-to-earth, no nonsense, practical help. She bathed Lucy and Hugh while I opened every suitcase wishing that I had been responsible for my own packing. I couldn't find matching pyjamas for anyone and there was a dearth of toothbrushes. The kind helper ran off in search of some. Meanwhile, the children all shared one toothbrush and fell into bed.

On the way to my room a small man had sidled up to me conspiratorially and said, "Breakfast television, BBC, 8.10am. Reception desk. OK?"

So the poor Hilton Hotel manager found himself fitting my electric hair rollers with a square-pin plug at two o'clock in the morning.

The next day we all rose at least half an hour before our 6.15am alarm call, except for Tom, whose 11th birthday it was. He slumbered on as his siblings fiddled with anything they could find in the hotel room.

"I want ITV, not BBC."

"Where's the colour gone?"

"What do you have to do to get a drink out of the fridge?"

"Look! Strawberries …"

There was a plate of fruit in the room – gold dust! Eventually, having by now emptied the contents of all eight suitcases, I found the semblance of a wardrobe for each child. Scrubbed and combed we went down to enjoy a real breakfast. I wasn't hungry but Tom ploughed solemnly through the works, anticipating boarding-school food later that day. Several strangers came up and said kind things to us. Then we discovered that we had made the front page of the *Daily Telegraph*.

"Is this embarrassing?" I vaguely asked.

"No, it's great," shouted Joe. "I can hardly wait to show everyone at school."

"Quite right. I have to book a car to take us."

I hadn't forgotten my assignment with the BBC but as I dashed back to our room, I collided with the small man again.

"I promise I'll be back at once, but I've no babysitter so what do I do?"

"Bring 'em, I suppose," he replied morosely.

So we all went, and the kids were lined up for an opening shot.

"This is boring," they kept saying.

I could see beads of sweat glistening on the small man's head.

I sat at a bogus breakfast table with a mug of weak tea. There was a policeman at the door.

"The plug in your ear will go dead when we go on air," said the sound engineer. It didn't; it emitted ghoulish shrieks, so I think I shouted to drown it out. Everyone was relieved when the interview was over.

I hoped there would be no bill to pay because the Office was taking care of us. As the wife of a public servant I should have known better. To my horror, it swallowed nearly all my loan, and I still had to pay for the taxi.

The *Daily Mirror* reporter was lurking. "What's your mother's address?"

"I'm sure your spies can work it out. I'm not going to tell you."

"You must be very hyped up," he said reflectively.

The BBC man came running. "We've just heard that the men are coming out of Libya today," he shouted.

I passed on the news to the other wives. "Believe it if you dare."

After fond farewells, and Happy Birthdays to Tom, we left. The sunshine was brilliant and the spring well advanced; it was a lovely time of year to come back home. Newspaper photographs had shown the police in St James's Square in shirtsleeves, licking ice cream cones. Now, as we drove along blossom-filled streets amongst brightly coloured cars, none of which was dented, Tripoli already seemed a long way off.

It took ages to get from Sussex to Oxford. Joe nagged: "Give me one good reason why I have to go to school today."

"You notice anything peculiar be'ind?" asked the driver. "I keep pulling over and I can't shake off that Mini. Reckon he's following us." Len Deighton flashed through my mind but I dismissed it as fanciful. No heroine of his would have tried evading a tail in a cumbersome minibus. She wouldn't have had four kids and eight bulging suitcases either. A number of reporters were waiting on my mother's front lawn. She opened the door.

"I've had a dreadful time," she said. "I'm exhausted, the phone never stops ringing and you'll have to go shopping for me this afternoon ..." In deference to her age I forbore to reply.

ITV evidently believed in reciprocity with the BBC as much as the Libyans did with the British. A car was waiting to whisk me to London for an interview on the 1pm ITV News. "I think we've missed it," the ITN driver said glumly and turning to my mother asked, "Mind if I phone?"

"Wipe your feet and don't take hours," commanded my mother. Half an hour later, I saw him proffering her a £1 note, which went smartly into the NSPCC tin.

Then a terrible thing happened. A reporter presented Tom with a beautiful BMX bike, complete with helmet and gloves. He was beaming happily for the first time in days, riding round and round the street. He had not much liked Libya.

I stared in horror. "But we can't accept that. We're public servants and can't be beholden to anyone."

"I've given it to Tom, not to you," the reporter pointed out.

Tom looked crestfallen: these things always happened to him.

"I'll ring the Office to check." I knew they would say "no" but there was no harm in trying.

I'd already phoned the Chief Clerk, the Head of Administration, and he had advised me not to have anything to do with the Press. Easier said than done, and anyway why not, I thought. They had been essential for my mental health over the last 10 days.

"Of course you can't accept it," he snapped and then added a bit more kindly, "I know it seems hard."

"I'll buy it," shouted my mother.

"It won't do," I shouted back.

Tom dismounted and handed the bike back. Then a bouquet arrived from the BBC: beautiful stocks, carnations, roses – all pink, white and mauve. I was glad I had made it clear that we could accept perishables of no significant value since the bicycle-giving journalists watched with interest as I accepted the flowers. That afternoon I delivered the boys to school and then in a daze of exhaustion went shopping for my mother. I could not resist buying three pounds of apples just in case they would not be available the next day. I had not yet shaken off Libya. I got back to hear confirmation of Oliver's arrival that night.

"We'll send a car for you to go to the airport," the ITV man informed me, still feeling one down on the BBC.

"Very kind, but I know Oliver wouldn't expect me to meet him and Gatwick is a good two and a half hours' drive. Sorry. Perhaps we've been married too long!" Or perhaps they were making a song-and-dance out of nothing.

In the 24 hours after the wives and children left, there had been frantic activity by the staff. As I had intimated to Sir John Leahy, they were convinced the Libyans would mess them about until the agreed final deadline of Sunday night. They feared that they would be moved to the airport well in advance of their flight, thus preventing them from finishing off the task of clearing the Office. (Indeed, they did leave the country 24 hours earlier than expected.)

After our departure they had discovered, possibly more by design than accident, a crate of champagne designated for the Queen's Birthday Party and had enjoyed that, mindful of their remaining duties. After an impromptu and incongruous supper with Juma, the Libyan fixer, Oliver had been able to go home for a good night's sleep. The staff had insisted that he should be rested so as to have his wits about him on the final day.

Two members of the Embassy staff were nominated to stay on in the British Interest Section of the Italian Embassy. This was unwelcome news. It had been hoped that this would not be necessary, or that new blood would be sent out from London. The two somewhat unwilling volunteers were Red Norton – who had been in Libya only a week, but was now entirely *au fait* with administration as a result of the intense practical experience he had undergone since his arrival – and George Anderson, the Consul.

George had argued against the need for a British Interest Section, but being professionals they accepted the inevitable. It was tough for them to be left to deal with an uncertain situation. They would live in the Residence – now pretty bare – and work in the Italian Embassy. The news was broken to their wives who were equally stunned, having eagerly anticipated their husbands' return.

The staff worked against the clock all night. There was the continuing task of shredding papers and smashing cipher and communication equipment and bagging it up for shipment to London. They also had to unravel previous travel arrangements and prepare to leave a day earlier than planned, though sceptical that the Libyans would actually let them go. It had been arranged that a special Trade Winds baggage flight would load on Friday 26 April, but as yet 40 tons of baggage (they hoped their estimate was correct) had not been removed to the airport. They had to ensure that the scheduled British Caledonian flight had room to transport them.

They had to brief the Italians on all sorts of administrative matters and show them the location of all the Embassy houses so that the hundreds of boxes of personal luggage could be collected. This was no mean feat since there were no addresses – only the larger streets had names, and no house had a number.

Throughout Saturday morning the British Caledonian flight was delayed so as to maximise the Embassy staff's working time. Finally the convoy set off, with Oliver in the leading flag car with the Italian *Chargé d'Affaires* and the ever-capable Signor Kardilli, sporting yet another elegant example of silk neckwear. To their amazement there was no airport delay. Oliver was delighted to discover that some significant Libyans had come to see him off.

There was Mr Miselati from Protocol Department and Mr Jerbi, with whom Oliver had negotiated throughout the crisis. This was an extremely decent gesture and despite the photographers trailing him, Mr Jerbi insisted on accompanying Oliver right to the airport steps and ostentatiously shaking hands. This was not just personally flattering, but a symbol of the Libyans' regret that diplomatic ties had been broken. Back in London Oliver told the Press that, "he had left Libya confident that he had made no enemies, but he had left them in no doubt as to the British Government's attitude".

We wanted to move back into our beloved Hampshire house but despite a break clause in the lease, the tenants refused to leave (court action would have taken months). The Press were fascinated to discover that for the first few nights we slept on my mother's floor. They and our friends were incredulous that we had been left without a roof over our heads. When Oliver explained to Geoffrey Howe, the Foreign Secretary, that we were homeless, he promised to do whatever he could to help.

I rented a house in an unpretentious neighbourhood of Oxford. The BBC seemed even more gobsmacked when they came to make a film of *A Day in the Life of* ... and found me hanging out the washing. I am always amused at the public perception of the diplomatic lifestyle.

One day a Fellow of Merton College – which was Oliver's *alma mater* – phoned to ask whether it would be advisable for him to accept an invitation to visit Libya. Seizing the moment I said:

"Before I fetch my husband I want to know if Merton has a property to let."

So for a year we lived in an ancient Oxford college house with a mediaeval wooden staircase, another fire hazard for me to fret over.

Lieutenant Colonel Barney Ferguson, the college bursar, a typically straightforward military man, asked about furniture and we repeated Geoffrey Howe's promise. After several weeks with nothing happening, Barney phoned again. "I'll ask Bicester Garrison for two sets of hard-stick furniture for a four-man quarter. You can pick it up after lunch."

The Press relentlessly questioned us about the fate of Hattie and Honeybun. I understand that a Sunday newspaper smuggled Honeybun into the UK, ignoring quarantine restrictions, and she was adopted by a beauty queen in Hemel Hemstead. Princess Antoinette arranged for Hattie to be shipped to Monaco where my brother-in-law, who was there on business, saw her reclining on a royal sofa.

Kate Adie made good her promise and the boys and I toured the BBC television studios. As soon as the tenants left I sold our Hampshire house. It saddened us all, especially as the trees we had planted had grown, but we wanted to continue living in Oxford.

The Office didn't want an unemployed Ambassador hanging about and Oliver, too, was impatient to get back to work. After some odd jobs in London, he went to New York (unaccompanied, as the FCO refused to pay for me), to cover the United Nations Autumn Assembly as a supernumerary Ambassador.

I was doing the ironing when the call came. It was Sir John Leahy again. "We've just posted your husband. Ambassador to Luxembourg."

"Luxembourg?"

"I assure you that it's a step to the highest echelons."

"Much," I thought and phoned Oliver in New York.

My mother said, "Your father used to be a representative at the Coal and Steel Community there. Very pretty place."

"But absolutely nothing to do."

"Well, I couldn't say. Jolly nice cakes, though."

AMBASSADORIAL ADVENTURES

The Residence in Luxembourg was a tall, 19th-century villa situated on the edge of the ravine that cuts across the city. There were electronically operated gates over which the Foreign Secretary Lord Carrington once climbed when the system failed, so they were obviously not very useful. For security reasons our predecessors had deemed it prudent to board up the ground floor, which remained creepily dark, so we lived on the first floor and above. Apart from the IRA, we could not imagine any other possible threat. Little did we know.

Oliver was soon an active Ambassador. Luxembourg, although tiny, held commercial interests for the UK in steel, television and banking. It is a member of the EU, NATO and the UN, so there was scope for political involvement. For four months each year, when the European Council was sitting, we were inundated by members of the British government, who used the Residence as a place to stay. They usually arrived in the dead of night, so we resorted to leaving notes directing them to beer and toothbrushes (the Foreign Secretary, Malcolm Rifkind, never remembered his). We admired how accurately they identified their allocated beds as we never heard any screams in the night.

Lucy attended the European School, which offered only morning lessons. There was little to occupy her in the afternoons. We were both lonely and purposeless. I joined every club I could find and forced myself to walk round Luxembourg City every day, including down into the manicured grassy Grund at the bottom of the ravine, with mini-golf and tourist train. I visited the European Court to listen to legal arguments over issues such as alcohol levels in beer. I even bought a bike.

Oliver had time on his hands and joined the 'Troatter Battien' (meaning 'The Guttersnipes'), a town band in which he played the flute and sported a spotted red neckerchief. They were enterprising enough to travel to Florida to play at weddings, and even performed at Disney World. "All the way from Luxembourg, West Germany," screamed the posters. At each venue a list of musicians was distributed. Halfway down, after Bottom the Weaver and Snug the Joiner was Oliver Miles, British Ambassador. But nobody ever noticed.

I had been warned that Mrs Thatcher, being Prime Minister, did not bother with diplomatic wives, but this was not true. I accompanied Oliver to greet her at the airport, expecting the cold shoulder. But my reputation from Libya had, I believe, reached her and she ran down the steps smiling broadly in my direction. She was neat, tailored, precise, and did not seem to like waste of any kind – including words, time or energy. I liked her immediately.

Within minutes of her arrival in Luxembourg we were chatting away and when we reached the Residence she asked for a tour. I showed her Hugh's bedroom – where Geoffrey Howe sometimes slept when Hugh was away. In the room was a pale-pink silk chaise-longue, on which Hugh – for want of a table – painted Dungeons and Dragons pieces. Mercifully, there was not a spot to be seen. Agreeing with me, she said that "the furnishings are probably too good for your children and my ministers".

After Mrs Thatcher had gone out, I tiptoed into her bedroom and saw a white satin negligee set hanging on the door. I looked at the label; it was Marks & Spencer. That confirmed my impression of her no-nonsense approach to life. At breakfast, she eyed Lucy, who was tucking into toast and marmalade.

"You look rather sticky," she said. "I think I'll sit over here if you don't mind."

On this occasion in February 1986, she and Geoffrey Howe had come for the signing of the Single European Act. They were both amicable guests, but Mrs T. evidently found Howe's lugubrious manner irritating.

"Don't just stand there, Geoffrey. Help me on with this thing," she remonstrated as she struggled with a shawl. She was pretty peremptory with Oliver, too. She could not decide whether to sign the Act or not and over a whisky nightcap they discussed the likely consequences. Oliver told her she should sign and she replied that it was none of his business. They continued to argue the following day as they drove in a bulletproof car to the Kirchberg, the site of the European institutions. Oliver remained adamant right up to the last minute. She signed.

As the cavalcade set off I remembered that Oliver had taken the car keys. I hopped into the last car and was swept along with the party, running to catch up as they moved swiftly to the conference chamber. I had no clearance or identification nor any idea where I was going. As I dashed along the corridors I encountered the German Chancellor, Helmut Kohl, who very politely stopped to say "Good morning" which slowed my progress, but I accomplished my mission and found my way out again without mishap.

From then on every visitor, official or not, asked whether they had slept in Mrs T's bed.

Alan Clark, the Minister of Trade, also stayed with us. After he left, the maid found a bulging envelope under his pillow, which she handed to me. Before sending it to his office I checked out the contents. They were the last thing I expected – photographs of old cars. In truth, I had very little idea either who Alan Clark was or his reputation. His visit meant just another effortful dinner party. So I was surprised a few years later when a friend phoned.

"I'm sorry to say you appear in, ahem, Alan Clark's diaries."

At least the Minister had not bothered to name us, although the chapter heading identified the post, but he did refer to Oliver as "that fucking Ambassador" and me as "his great plain wife". He complained about my short-sightedness in not providing Radox for his bath whereas there had been a choice of whiskies in his room. Oliver said I had probably upset him by greeting him as a fellow EU sceptic while he was on pro-EU business.

In the large sterile-looking Residence kitchen, I was somewhat perplexed to discover a deep fat fryer which could cook 40 kilos of chips from frozen. I could not envisage a use for such a gadget since we weren't the Belgian Embassy. Although we were allocated only three dozen plates, we rejoiced in a plate warmer for 200. I gave up trying to follow London's logic. At last I had been given a proper staff: three maids and a cook. This was much better than Libya where we had to recruit people willing to endure the tribulations of Tripoli. In Luxembourg, the mediocre cook was Jean, who Lucy witnessed blowing his nose on the tea towels. He took revenge by putting a stick in her shoe on St Nicholas Day, when good children receive presents. I remain most grateful to him for taking me stock car racing which livened up Sundays no end.

There were only two British diplomats in Luxembourg. The wife of the other one briefly brightened my life when she hoaxed the local Press on April Fools' Day and caused a real upset. The first year the newspapers carried the shock-horror story that the ravine was to be flooded; Luxembourg City would resemble Geneva with pleasure boats and lakeside cafés. The following year the Press announced that the Turner painting the British government had presented to the Luxembourg government was a fake. This caused more consternation in London than amongst the Luxembourgers, who gave no public reaction.

Her successor, bar one, arrived newly married and anticipating a lifestyle she quickly discovered did not exist. One day she burst in unannounced and told Oliver in no uncertain terms and at the top of her voice, what he could do with his horrible Embassy. She then left the country.

One Saturday Oliver and the children were driving through the centre of town when they were horrified to see the old cathedral spire, largely constructed of wood, filled with flames. They watched as it toppled to the ground. The official explanation was that workmen restoring the building were responsible, and that might have been the end of it. However a few weeks afterwards, the 'Luxembourg Bomber' began his activities and held the country in thrall for almost a year. He was never identified but it was rumoured that he was a disaffected policeman.

One of his early exploits was to blow up an electricity pylon which he had booby trapped, so injuring investigators. One afternoon an eerie silence descended as police responded to a warning (false, as it happened), that the bridge nearest to our house would be destroyed. The bomber's biggest escapade was to blow up the city gas works under cover of the Grand Duke's birthday fireworks display. This terror contrasted markedly with Luxembourg's image as a European administration and banking centre and sleepy rural idyll.

On the evening of Monday 29 May 1985, Oliver on flute, I on piano and an Austrian violinist, Francis Rosner, were about to practise a piano trio in the privacy of the Residence sitting room. As we tuned up, the phone rang.

I lifted the receiver. There was a moment's pause and then a threatening foreign voice said, "Switch on your TV right away or it will be the worse for you."

The man rang off before Oliver could intervene.

The phone rang again.

"You go this time," I said.

He came back, looking puzzled.

"It was someone talking Italian as if he was reading a recipe book. Very strange."

"Perhaps we had better do what he said and switch on the telly."

The pictures told the story. Trouble had arisen at Brussels' Heysel Stadium between Liverpool fans and the Italian supporters of Juventus. Just before kick-off, Liverpool fans had invaded the Italian terraces and fighting ensued. As we watched the live coverage, horrified, the mounted Belgian police remained strangely immobile. That night, 39 fans died and 600 people were injured, mostly Italian. While we were taking in this ghastly scene, the phone rang every few minutes and Oliver was getting up and down to answer it.

"It seems to be mainly Italians, furious with us, but as I can't understand much, I am unsure how to help."

"I'll answer," I said, apprehensively picking up another call and bracing myself for the onslaught.

A very loud and fruity English voice said, "I'd like to speak to the British Ambassador."

Oliver was showing Francis to the door. "Perhaps I can help?" I said.

"Perhaps you can," he replied sarcastically. "Perhaps you can tell me why the British Embassy encouraged me to bring my theatre company to this city where there is no audience?"

I thought I was going bonkers. "I'm sorry but I don't know about this. Could I ask who you are, please?"

"Derek Nimmo, of course. Everything is set up at the Hotel Continental and only half a dozen people have turned up. I have to speak to the Ambassador."

"Before you do, Mr Nimmo, I should tell you that there seems to be a crisis over a football match in Belgium which has had an impact here."

"What's that got to with me?"

"Or any of us. But that is what is happening."

He paused. "I suppose you will be coming to see the show."

"Of course. Here's Oliver."

A few minutes later, I asked what was going on.

"There are a lot of Italian immigrants resident here who are presumably the ones phoning us. As for Derek Nimmo, well,

I'm afraid I failed to tell you he was coming with some play the name of which I've forgotten."

"But you know how much I miss live theatre."

"Do you really want to watch a farce at the Continental Hotel?"

"We haven't any option now. We've got to smooth Derek Nimmo's feathers."

"If you say so. Oh dear, the phone again. Are they going to keep us up all night?"

It was probably not 6.30am when one of the maids burst into our bedroom. "Quick!" she screamed. "Get up. The Red Brigade have put a bomb in the house."

We leapt out of bed. Lucy appeared in her pyjamas. "Why is she screaming, Mummy?"

"Oh, don't worry, she's just had a silly idea. Let's go and have breakfast."

Oliver's bodyguard, a perfumed hunk called Serge, arrived and there were some low-voiced consultations.

"I'm pretty sure it's a hoax, but keep your eyes and ears open, and phone me if you're worried," Oliver told me.

"Do the police know?"

"They're the ones saying it's a hoax. I must get on. Bye, Lucy."

The day proceeded normally. I booked seats for Wednesday night's performance. The phone rang intermittently. Sometimes it was the creepy recipe-reader and sometimes a more serious caller expressing concern at the supine stance of the British Embassy. My stock reply was that the action was in Brussels, not here. One British newspaper columnist wondered why there had been no backlash anywhere. I wish he had asked me. Derek Nimmo graciously phoned to apologise "in case I was rude last night". He had just read the local paper and was beginning to see what was going on. I told him we were seeing his show the following evening and held out an olive branch:

"Would you like to come to a buffet lunch on Friday and talk to the British community? They would love to meet you."

"Delighted. You can tell me what you thought of the show."

I did not want to leave Lucy on Wednesday night in such

a shaky atmosphere and instructed the maids to phone Serge, who would be glued to Oliver's side, if there were any developments. They ignored me. When we returned from the show the Luxembourg police had just carried out a thorough search of the house, acting on a tip-off. Lucy was inconsolable.

"I want to go home. I don't like it here."

Privately, I agreed with her. "It's OK, darling," I held her tight. "The policemen just came to see that we were safe."

Friday came. Chairs were placed in the garden under an overcast sky for the Nimmo presentation. Oliver flew to London for talks over the weekend, and Serge went home.

Then the Red Brigade called to say there were bombs in the house and that they would explode shortly. I wondered whether my *blasé* disregard of this warning was irresponsible. I sat at the back of the audience and imagined tomorrow's headlines.

Derek Nimmo did his act: "I'm sure you've all heard this story, do stop me if so … it was when I was dressed as a monk in the Vatican and got shopped by a nun … You haven't heard it before? … Oh, good …" He had the audience hanging on every word and roaring with laughter. We ate lunch and I complimented him on the show. He said his troupe was heading for the Gulf and all sorts of unknown dangers. I refrained from mentioning that he might at that very moment be sitting on a bomb.

Everyone, staff included, departed for the weekend, and a silence fell upon the large old house. Lucy and I were alone. I tried to be jolly as we went to the market the next morning but everything felt oppressive. At tea-time on Sunday we returned from a walk in the countryside. I was putting on the kettle when my heart skipped a beat at the sound of the doorbell. The intercom screen showed a man climbing over the wall.

"Quick, Lucy," I said. "Go and press the alarm in the bedroom. I'll watch where he goes."

She clung to me, crying. So together we ran upstairs, pressed the panic button, then raced back down to the kitchen monitor. But there was no sign of the intruder. That was a bad moment as he could already be in the house. Then I heard sirens followed by rattling and hammering on the roof and doors as the police swarmed over the house. Lucy was screaming with fear. I did not want us to be shot and decided the safest place would be the entrance hall. We stood hugging each other as numerous officers, guns cocked, swarmed through the house. Then the officer in charge approached me, shaking his head.

"What did you think you saw?" He seemed sceptical, if not downright rude. When I told him he replied, "Madame, I think it is possible you are a lady of *'un certain age'* as we say."

That put the lid on it. After our mid-tour leave I decided to remain in Oxford and do my professional social work training. So Lucy and I took up residence in our newly acquired Victorian house with only a sheet of blue plastic between us and the elements, while the builders worked at a leisurely pace through the winter of 1986 to make the place habitable. There was, however, a difficulty. If I was deemed absent from post, Oliver's allowances would be cut and the children would have to leave their schools. So Lucy and I commuted, sometimes driving the 500-odd miles and sometimes flying, so as to hang on to these allowances. It was quite exhilarating to be hosting a diplomatic dinner in Luxembourg one night and sitting in an Oxford Poly classroom the next morning, looking as if butter wouldn't melt in my mouth.

Lucy was now seven years old and able to start school in Oxford. This was a great improvement since she was fully occupied all day. She began to settle down and make friends after all the upheavals she had experienced in her short life. I was also able to keep in closer contact with the boys, all of whom were boarding in or near Oxford. In the vacation either Oliver came back on leave or we returned to Luxembourg. In July 1988 I gained my social-work diploma and found a job. And, after serving more than three years in Luxembourg, Oliver requested a home posting. "Sure," replied the man in Personnel Department. "You're off to Belfast."

Lucy and I flew to Belfast shortly after Oliver, wondering how much more insecurity we could tolerate. Oliver had been allocated a small, detached house in Helen's Bay just outside the city, surrounded by high fuschia hedges. A bit too high, I thought, as he searched the underside of his Ford Fiesta for bombs.

In Belfast city centre I was appalled by the numbers of armed police and military Land Rovers, and at being searched just to go into Marks & Spencer. In 1988, the terror level was unremitting and a high-profile incident occurred almost every week. It was at this time that three Provisional IRA men, subsequently found to be unarmed, were shot dead in Gibraltar by the SAS on suspicion of planning to attack British soldiers.

This incident prompted a chain of events: at Milltown Cemetery Michael Stone opened fire on the mourners at the funeral of the three men killed in Gibraltar. Then two British soldiers drove into the funeral procession for one of Stone's victims (by mistake, it appeared), and were shot dead by the IRA. There seemed no end to the violence. At the end of the week I told Oliver that neither Lucy nor I could face two years living in such an atmosphere.

So Oliver decided to commute each week from Oxford to work at Stormont, the seat of the Northern Irish Parliament. In a secure bunker, he engaged in negotiations with his Irish Ambassadorial counterpart over issues arising from the Anglo-Irish Agreement, which had recently been signed by Mrs Thatcher and Garret FitzGerald.

Every Monday at dawn a taxi collected Oliver to take him to Heathrow airport. Occasionally a kind Minister would invite him to share his private jet instead, leaving from RAF Lyneham. One Monday, I heard an unusually agitated driver with a thick foreign accent arguing with Oliver downstairs. They eventually left and I snoozed until the doorbell rang. An RAF driver stood smartly on the step expecting to collect Oliver. We stared at each other in horror. Who had collected him earlier? After taking the dog for a walk I contacted the police, who, hearing we had been in Libya, jumped into action and discovered Oliver, unaware of the panic, enjoying VIP treatment. All became clear: the taxi firm had sent a driver as usual and the noisy negotiation arose from Oliver's request to go to Wiltshire, rather than to Heathrow.

The Oxford police – now aware of our Libyan connection – insisted on logging us onto their high-alert system for extra protection, overriding our protest that it was unnecessary. Soon after, they reported a suspicious car outside our house with an 'L' registration plate. Trying not to laugh we explained that it was our car, and that the 'L' denoted Luxembourg, not Libya. That same car made difficulties for me when I was on a student placement in Bicester Probation Office. Besides the nefarious 'L', it also sported CD plates which generated some hostility and bullying behaviour from some of the other staff. It was intimated that I would be denied my qualification because I was regarded as a toff. At the end of my time a little goodbye party was given and I was presented with a small china pot of flowers which, to my mind, confirmed their unassailable view of me. On the way home, I stopped off at the Oxfam shop and handed it in.

After his two-year stint in Belfast, Oliver was made the Economic, Trade and Aid Under-Secretary in the FCO in London. Despite being given political jobs he had always been interested in commercial matters. so it was an exciting development when the government decided to promote exports by building a close liaison between the Department of Trade and the FCO, under a new body called the Joint Directorate. Oliver headed this under the auspices of Michael Heseltine, the President of the Board of Trade. The family derived some amusement when Oliver was asked to join a panel to choose prizewinning designs of nightwear and lingerie. These were then modelled at a dinner in the presence of Princess Anne, who was Patron of the British Knitting and Clothing Export Council.

That same year, Mrs Thatcher asked Oliver to organise the 1990 NATO summit. And two years later at very short notice he was bounced into setting up the London Conference on Yugoslavia.

The Prime Minister, John Major wrote:

"Dear Oliver

I fear that last week at the London Conference you paid the price of success. Had you not organised the NATO summit so well, you would not have been roped in for this one. You did nothing to undermine, and everything to enhance, your reputation as an organiser of Conferences ..."

Fortunately, this long stay at home gave me the opportunity to finally start my career. I was somewhat annoyed to discover there might have been even more. One evening we were dining in St Antony's College and one of the Fellows remarked that he had been rather perplexed that Oliver had never responded to their invitation to have a year's visiting Fellowship at the college.

"We sent a message through the Foreign Office when you left Libya."

"It wasn't in their interest so it never reached us," I said.

After I qualified as a social worker I took a maternity-cover social work job at the John Radcliffe Hospital, moving to the Nuffield Orthopaedic Centre six months later. At the same time I enrolled in a year's introductory course in psychotherapy at the Oxford University Institute of Psychiatry.

This stood me in good stead when in 1992 I moved on to work as a probation officer. This had always been my aim, and I loved it. But the day my confirmation came through I shocked my line manager by handing in my notice. The bell had tolled again. Oliver was being sent abroad for one last time. Poor Lucy was bundled off to boarding school, and we returned to Athens.

The Last Post

As a teenager I had a strange experience. My father took the family to Greece, where he was working, and a colleague of his offered to tell my fortune in coffee grounds. I laughed when he, peering into the tiny cup, predicted marriage to a diplomat who would become Ambassador in Paris. He was not quite correct because the man I married ended up, ironically, as Ambassador in Athens. But it was accurate enough to make me wonder.

In 1993, we arrived at the magnificent British Embassy Residence in Kolonaki in the heart of Athens. The domestic staff lined up in Edwardian style to greet us, which was very humbling. The Office was a short walk from the house across the garden. Our predecessor told me that he had picked up a bullet lying on the garden path as he walked to work one morning. It was never explained.

The huge house had a number of antiques and pictures. Accompanying them was an official list denoting the order in which items and personnel should be saved in the event of fire. First was the original Thomas Phillips' portrait of Byron, hanging in the drawing room. Second was the Ambassador himself. Third was the set of four antique wooden hall chairs. In fourth place, came the Ambassador's wife and family.

The Residence had a unique set of silver cutlery engraved with the initials of Edward VIII, which the butler, Sergeant Hasler, counted meticulously before and after every dinner party. He then spent hours the next morning chasing up teaspoons taken by guests as 'souvenirs'. When London requested that we return the valuable set, I was relieved that he had taken such care that not one piece was missing.

Since our first posting to Athens, Greece had entered the European Union and was rapidly being transformed into a viable modern nation. Greece took over the Presidency of the EU while we were there, which meant we travelled to Corfu for the Council of European Ministers. Oliver and I were having a late evening swim in the hotel pool with Sarah Hogg, who was head of the Prime Minister's Policy Unit. I was reminding her that as students we had worked together in Fenwicks' lingerie department, when John Major, the Prime Minister, hailed us from his top-floor window but declined our shouted invitation to come down for a dip.

Greece was not high on official visitors' lists at that time but the Archbishop of Canterbury and Mrs Carey did stay for a few days while ecumenical talks were held with leaders of the Greek Orthodox Church. One morning I raced downstairs before breakfast in my nightdress to find six orthodox priests sitting silently in the drawing room. On seeing me, they rose up as one, identically dressed in chimney-pot hats, like targets at a coconut shy. The Careys were invited to walk in the mountains by their Greek hosts. Oliver offered to lend them some warm jackets. After they had set off I discovered the Archbishop was wearing my Barbour which was in current use and whose pocket was full of Tampax.

One afternoon and with only 10 minutes' notice, such was the security, we were told that Peter Ustinov, as Chancellor of Durham University, would be awarding an honorary doctorate to Mikhail Gorbachov, and that he would be accompanied by Raisa. We arrived late and were ushered into the front row. Peter Ustinov was in full flow and full fig, with a gold tassel swinging over his right eye and an encrusted academic gown adorning his fine frame. While he eulogised, my knees were pressed hard against Mr Gorbachov's with nowhere to move them, even had I wanted to. I felt it was a bit much to stare at him from such a short distance. Any hope of speaking to him afterwards was frustrated as the party was whisked away before the clapping stopped.

A perk of the post was that we were extremely spoiled by wealthy Greeks, who each summer weekend escorted us to inaccessible islands aboard their luxury yachts. One of these kind people was Stelios Hadjioannou's elderly father, who owned a tanker fleet. He introduced us to his son whom I later met at a party in London. "I'm going to start a new airline, what do you think? Will it work?" he asked me.

Quick as a flash I replied, "No, it will be a total disaster. Look what happened to Freddie Laker." (Laker's 'no-frills' airline went bust in 1982.) Stelios evidently did not rate my business acumen very highly because he went on to found the cheap air-travel company Easyjet which in 2013, was valued at over six billion pounds.

A music festival was held annually in my favourite town, Nafplion, in the Peloponnese. On one visit we heard Nicolai Gedda and Victoria de Los Angeles sing. Afterwards someone said, "It's Madame de Los Angeles's birthday and we have a cake. Do join us. She would be disappointed if you didn't." So with a dozen fans, in some far-away garden at one o'clock in the morning, we sang "Happy Birthday, Victoria". She was 80 that day.

We were invited to the wedding of the year. The bride was the daughter of the ship owner, George Livanos. An evening reception for 2,000 guests was to be held in the garden of their house outside Athens. Unseasonable rain poured down all afternoon. Seating plans had been drawn up and tables beautifully laid but all were dragged quickly under cover. When they were set out again the name cards and table numbers were all muddled up. Various divorced couples ended up on the same tables, which caused some gossip and amusement. It took quite a time to find our table but eventually 12 of us sat down. Oliver was enjoying chatting up a young woman with long blonde hair who was sitting next to him, when a note was passed to me from another table. It read: "Please tell your husband he is talking to the wife of an IRA hitman."

One of Oliver's objectives was to raise Britain from fifth to fourth trading partner with Greece. He had already successfully completed a British commercial and cultural promotion in Luxembourg; now he envisaged a more ambitious, festival called 'Britain in Greece' (BiG). The job of administrator was full time for a year, but the salary was nominal. After a number of PR companies rejected the terms, Oliver drew a blank. I had been biding my time. "I could do it," I said.

The Embassy allocated me a part-time secretary and a room with a telephone. My job was to create something out of nothing. Oliver was busy raising £1million to finance the festival and found nine patrons and 12 sponsors to put up the money which I placed in an account earning 14 percent interest, so after all expenses had been met I still had £30,000 to finance another 'BiG', earmarked to take place in two years' time.

The British Council was my big ally. John Munby, the director in Greece, had already booked the Philharmonia Orchestra under Evgeny Svetlanov and the Nottingham Playhouse's production of *The Tempest*, and I wanted to build on that. The Embassy commercial secretary suggested Stomp, an alternative dance company using ironmongery as instruments. They performed to wildly enthusiastic audiences in the ancient Herodou Atticou Theatre in Athens.

With an opening ball, lectures, exhibitions, poetry readings, children's activities, a Trade Fair and sports (including the Oxford and Cambridge Boat Race teams competing against a Greek team on a lake in northern Greece), there was a lot to organise. The day I booked two Routemaster open-top buses to drive overland from London to Athens I had to negotiate in English and French because of their intended route, and Greek because I needed garaging and and cleaning facilities.

"I'm putting in for a pay rise," I teased Oliver. "You didn't specify multiple languages in my contract."

"Do you have a contract?"

One bus broke down in Italy but after an agonising delay they both appeared on the Athens streets and were an instant attraction. BiG companies covered them with advertising, and they filled with school children, who wanted to ride upstairs and touch the overhanging trees. (I was disconcerted to discover that there were also some low-hanging power lines). The Greek ex-Foreign Minister telephoned Oliver early the first morning to say that he couldn't believe his eyes when he saw a London double-decker whizz past his bathroom window.

A reclusive media millionaire, Christos Lambrakis, whom Oliver had failed to entice early on in his search for sponsors, contacted us when he fully appreciated what a huge initiative BiG was. Besides giving us free advertising in his magazines and newspapers, he projected a prominent BiG flyer onto the outside wall of the Megaron, the newly built concert hall where some of our events were to be held. As a thank you to him I asked our celebrity chef, Claire Macdonald, to make his favourite pudding – Atholl brose – which consists of oats, cream, whisky and honey. After she had left I searched every fridge in the Residence. The butler said to me gloomily:

"If you're looking for that stuff Lady Macdonald left, Leonidas threw it out. He thought it was vomit."

The Red Arrows came and, helped by the military and naval sections of the Embassy, I negotiated the complete clearance of shipping and air routes over Piraeus harbour for an afternoon. On the last night of the festival, we mounted a grand firework display from the Royal Yacht *Britannia*. (The Royal Family was not present out of consideration for the exiled King Constantine.) The Royal Marine band, as always, brought tears to our eyes as they Beat the Retreat.

The Residence staff was tireless and nothing short of brilliant throughout the entire festival. They coped with a full contingent of VIP visitors, and we held open house at lunchtime every day for three weeks. One lunch included a University Chancellor, a detective from Leeds Constabulary, three students from the Royal Academy of Music, a honky-tonk pianist called Terry White, and Jeremy Isaacs, General Director of the Royal Opera House. Suddenly Jeremy yelled down the table to the honky-tonk pianist: "Do you know *Father*

Used a Pin to get his Winkle Out?" and they proceeded to sing a duet.

As he took his leave, the Detective Sergeant told Oliver in his broad Yorkshire accent, "I wouldn't have credited it if I hadn't witnessed it with my own two eyes." His departure coincided with the theft of valuable goods from the Design Museum exhibition in another part of Athens. A great opportunity to demonstrate professional policing methods to the Greek constabulary was sadly lost.

Hansard, the official report of the House of Commons, records that on 25 October 1995 David Davis, Minister of State, FCO, congratulated us on BiG's success in a Commons debate on Britain's relationship with Greece:

"For two (sic) weeks in September and October this year, Greece was treated to one of the biggest celebrations of British culture and achievement ever seen in that country. This was the 'Britain in Greece' festival … I should like to pay tribute to the work of our Ambassador in Greece and his wife – Oliver and Julia Miles – and to the director of the British Council in Athens, John Mundy (sic) and all their staffs, who put such energy into masterminding the hugely successful project of raising Britain's profile in Greece … The rich menu of events and spectacle was cultural diplomacy at its best …"

As decreed by the FCO, Oliver had to retire on his 60th birthday. At Christmas, we gave the dreaded 'servants ball' for the whole staff and their families, which on this occasion turned into a celebration and jamboree. BiG had taken the Greeks by surprise and they had reacted with generosity and enthusiasm. We thought we were leaving on a high note but there was a sting in the tail. Just as homage was being paid to a popular retiring Ambassador, a crisis blew up in the Aegean which could have sparked a war between Greece and Turkey.

It started when a Turkish freighter ran aground on some rocks in the Aegean, and the Greek lifeboat rescued the crew. A Turkish journalist was dared to plant a Turkish flag on one of the rocky islets called Imia (Greek) or Kardak (Turkish). As a result, aircraft and warships on both sides were mobilised.

Since both countries are members of NATO, other NATO members – the US, the UK, and oddly, Germany – were called on to restrain both parties and broker peace. The message sent to all three member countries arrived at dead of night, but it was Oliver who found his way to Mr Pangalos, the Greek Foreign Minister and using his fluent Greek, urged him to desist from military action. A similar message was sent to Mr Baykal in Turkey. In the end, both sides climbed down. By the time Malcolm Rifkind, the British Foreign Secretary, arrived in Athens, the crisis had been averted.

Many Greeks accused Oliver of not supporting their cause. It was alarming to see how quickly the appreciation for all that he had done evaporated. One Greek soldier's mother publicly declared she would rather her son died than the Greeks should give up their territorial claims. Oliver was robust in his defence of the British position and by the time we left, honour had been satisfied. But it left a nasty taste.

The night before we left, I attended the opera *Wozzeck* at the Megaron, which was sung in German. While that language defeated me I was chuffed to find that I was able to understand the subtitles written in Greek.

So on 6 March, 1996 having been wined and dined by colleagues and friends all over Greece and packed our stuff including two roomsful of farewell presents, we left for Patras to start the long drive home. The butler asked me whether I would miss diplomatic life. I said that although I regretted leaving Greece, I was thrilled to have my freedom. But it was sad to reflect on how much of the children's early lives we had missed.

We were going home via Venice. Meeting the Italian Military Attaché, Luca, in Athens a few weeks before our departure, I told him our plans and asked prosaically where we might park our car in Venice. He offered to make the necessary arrangements. We heard nothing, until news broke that Luca and the Dutch Military Attaché were being expelled, having been found *in flagrante* on an official trip. I was puzzled until I discovered that the Dutch Military Attaché was female.

I was reluctant to trouble Luca with my parking problem while he was contending with bigger issues, but in the end he turned up trumps. When we disembarked in Venice, a tall, handsome *carabaniero* greeted us, adorned in a long cape to keep out the biting wind and rain. He insisted on garaging the car and escorting us to our hotel on the *vaporetto*.

A wealthy Greek friend who was active in the campaign to save Venice from flooding had arranged for us to dine with a prominent American who owned a palazzo on the Grand Canal. Whisked back into a Henry James atmosphere, we spent a delightful evening in glittering company. Then the Tory grandees, Sir Alistair and Lady MacAlpine, transported us in their motor launch to our hotel through the silent city lapped by oily black water and lit by platinum moonlight.

And that was the last magical moment of Oliver's – and my – diplomatic career.

EPILOGUE

B efore Oliver retired I thought a lot about life after diplomacy and how it would affect us. There was no cascade of job offers as I had hoped so he joined a group of Middle East consultants from which his current writing of a daily global newsletter on Middle Eastern current affairs has evolved. He became deputy chairman of the Libyan British Business Council promoting trade with Libya, which meant a number of trips back there. Together we were treated to several Swan Hellenic cruises with Oliver as a guest lecturer.

On 27 April 2004, Oliver orchestrated an open letter (prompted by our son Tom and me) addressed to the-then Prime Minister, Tony Blair, signed by 52 former Ambassadors and High Commissioners. The letter drew attention to Blair's too-close cooperation with the United States over the Arab-Israel problem and Iraq. As a result of that and our profile in Libya, he continues to appear regularly in the media.

I rejoined the Probation Service. One of its most satisfying aspects was the opportunity to get to know people over a period of time and at a meaningful level which I believe is the way to rehabilitate offenders. This is in marked contrast to the Diplomatic model of 'shake hands and pass on'. Since qualifying as a psychotherapist in 2003 I have worked amongst other places as a therapist in two men's prisons, and with drug and alcohol users. Currently I run a private practice.

In 1988, I instigated the reopening of the Oxford Playhouse which had gone dark. I now revel in drama, music and ballet and the availability of books, television and radio, all of which I sorely missed during almost three decades of foreign postings. As our tally of grandchildren reaches double figures it seems no month goes by without a plethora of excitements that require diary-keeping to meticulous Diplomatic Service standards. I cherish my freedom. And I have my own front door.

I raise three cheers to all the diplomatic wives who keep the home fires burning, the flag flying and who don't go off their heads while in vassalage to the Foreign Office.

ACKNOWLEDGEMENTS

I would like to thank Dan Hiscocks, Martha Ellen Zenfell and Jenny Orr of Eye Books for all their sympathetic support and indispensable help in bringing this book to fruition. I owe a huge debt of gratitude to my brother Edmund Weiner and to friends Ann Pasternak-Slater and Karen McNicoll for all the many and various roles they have undertaken during the gestation period. Thanks, too, to my daughter-in-law Samantha Suissa for her early cover designs. It goes without saying that without Oliver and his demanding career there would have been no material, and without the kids far fewer dramas and laughs. I also have to thank the drip feed of dozens of people who, over the years, have nagged me to 'write it down'. And that leads me to acknowledge my mother's wisdom in preserving the letters on which so much of this tale is based.

ABOUT EYE BOOKS

www.eye-books.com

Eye Books is a small independent publishing house. The team who works at Eye Books passionately believes that the more you put into life the more you get out of it.

Eye Books celebrates 'living' rather than existing. We publish stories that show ordinary people can and do achieve extraordinary things.

We are committed to ethical publishing and try to minimise our carbon footprint in the manufacturing and distribution of all Eye Books.

Follow Eye Books on Facebook, Twitter @eyebooks and our website www.eye-books.com